A STEP-BY-STEP
GUIDE TO
USABILITY TESTING

A STEP-BY-STEP GUIDE TO USABILITY TESTING

Peter P. Mitchell, Ph.D., CHFP
Research Assistant Professor

University of Miami, Miller School of Medicine
The Center for Patient Safety
Miami, Florida

University of Miami
Department of Psychology
Coral Gables, Florida

iUniverse, Inc.
New York Lincoln Shanghai

A Step-by-Step Guide to Usability Testing

iUniverse books may be ordered through booksellers or by contacting:

iUniverse
2021 Pine Lake Road, Suite 100
Lincoln, NE 68512
www.iuniverse.com
1-800-Authors (1-800-288-4677)

ISBN-13: 978-0-595-42276-0 (pbk)
ISBN-13: 978-0-595-86668-7 (cloth)
ISBN-13: 978-0-595-86613-7 (ebk)
ISBN-10: 0-595-42276-4 (pbk)
ISBN-10: 0-595-86668-9 (cloth)
ISBN-10: 0-595-86613-1 (ebk)

Printed in the United States of America

Introduction

- A quotation from Krug (2000), "If you want a great site, you've got to test." The reference here is to the design of websites, however, the same quote applies to any new software application, a new medical device, and new consumer product, and so on. Technology-based products are complex, and they rarely, if ever, get built correctly on the first pass. You simply must conduct "ease-of-use" testing to make sure your new software (or new product) will be acceptable to the marketplace.

- Most companies are finding that Usability Testing is simply something they have to have not just to make sure their product is usable, but to make sure they do not get crushed by the competition. If your competition has a product/software application that is superior to yours on the metric of "ease-of-use", you are in trouble. There is no sensible new product manager in this country that would develop a new high-tech product without including Usability Testing as part of the development process. And funds to do this research are always included in the budget. It's as simple as that.

- A Usability Testing program can be, but does not have to be, a difficult or expensive undertaking. Each chapter in this book provides step-by-step directions to carry out effective Usability Testing.

- The difference between this book and others on this topic is that this book provides you with just the information you need to know to get your Usability Testing program up and going quickly. And A Step-by-Step Guide to Usability Testing provides you with a simple roadmap to follow. The book uses as few words as possible to give you the instructions you need to get the job done.

About This Book

- <u>A Step-by-Step Guide to Usability Testing</u> is a book designed for the person who is new to the widely-used technique of Usability Testing. In some organizations one individual, or a small team of people, are handed the job of being the usability experts for the company. This book is designed for these people.

- The same Usability Testing methods are used regardless if one is evaluating a website, a new software application, a new consumer product, a new medical device, or a new IVR (interactive voice response) telephony system.

- Usability is all about making things easy to use. If you follow the step-by-step directions and the Checklists at the end of each chapter, you will most certainly enhance the ease-of-use of your website (or your software, your hardware, etc).

- From the findings from this testing you will obtain specific recommendations to improve the user interface of your website or your new product. The content of the book is directed to the person who will be the Moderator within your company, or the person that will be managing the project if you use an outside Moderator to run the Usability Testing. This book is, in effect, a "Quick Reference Card" for Usability Testing. It covers the specific DOs and DON'Ts of Usability Testing.

- There are a few conventions I have used in the book. Researchers often speak of the test "subject". The American Psychological Association recommends the term test "Participants", which is the term I use throughout this book. I have capitalized certain words that are key components of Usability Testing, such as the "Screener" and the "Tasks" and the "Questionnaire", etc. This is done in order to make these terms stand out. The part of any product that the end user actually sees and touches is the "user interface", sometimes referred to as the "UI".

- I strongly urge everyone who conducts research with human Participants to follow all of the requirements of the Institutional Review Board (IRB) of their organization and follow all of the guidelines established by the HSRO (Human Participants Research Office) of their institution. To obtain information on these institutions simply type "IRB" into any major search engine. Also, The Human Factors and Ergonomics Society also has a Code of Ethics, which is given in the Appendix of the book. I expect that anyone conducting any research with human Participants will carefully follow the rules and guidelines of each of these regulatory bodies in order to properly protect all test Participants at all times.

- I genuinely hope that the procedures and recommendations covered in this book will assist you in making your company's products and services easier to use.

Contents

Chapter	Page
1 The Usability Testing Questions to Ask Yourself	1
2 How to Determine Whether or Not Usability Testing Is Needed	6
3 How to Develop the Test Plan	9
4 How to Create the Tasks	13
5 How to Develop the User Profile—The Screener	17
6 How to Develop the Moderator's Guide and Probe Questions	20
7 How to Develop the Data Logging Form	22
8 How to Develop the Post-test Questionnaire	28
9 How to Recruit Your Test Participants	31
10 How to Arrange for an Outside Test Facility	35
11 How to Set-up the Usability Testing Rooms and the Video Equipment	39
12 How to Conduct the Usability Testing Sessions	42
13 How to Perform the Necessary Statistical Tests	50
14 How to Present Results for Maximum Impact	57
15 How to Act On the Results: Making User Interface Design Changes	60
16 Training the Usability Testing Moderator	64
17 Online Usability Testing	69
18 Working with the Institutional Review Board (IRB) at Your Institution	71

Appendices

Appendix   **Page**

A   A Sample Test Plan 73

B   Example of a Screener 76

C   Sample Testing Schedules 79

D   Sample Tasks 80

E   Sample Rating Scales 83

F   Sample Introduction Sheet 85

G   Sample Moderator's Guide and Probe Questions 86

H   Examples of a Post-test Questionnaire 88

I   An Example Executive Summary in a Report 90

J   Sample Video Permission & Confidentiality Form .92

K   Code of Ethics When Conducting Usability Testing 93

L   List of Professional Societies 95

M   List of Usability Testing Consultants 96

N   List of Resources for Recruiting Participants & Renting a Testing Facility . . .97

O   Acknowledgements 103

P   Bio for the Author 104

Q   Workshop At Your Company 106

R   References 107

CHAPTER 1

The Usability Testing Questions to Ask Yourself

I. Why bother with Usability Testing? Simple: The ROI is very compelling
Usability Testing has shifted from being a "nice to have" to a "must have" in the development of a new website, a software product, or a new piece of hardware. It is simply too risky to launch a new product without it. This is true in virtually all large corporations, healthcare institutions, and government units within the United States. What began as a campaign to help make the user's/consumer's experience on a website or with a certain software application be as pleasant as possible has turned into a situation that if you do not have a human factors team (or usability specialists) as part of the core product development group for a new product, there is a very good chance that your product will be soundly beaten in the marketplace by a competitor who did pay attention to the "usability details". More than one career has ended as a result of a manager failing to understand this need.

The usability improvement process has three distinct needs: (a) user needs analysis and Task analysis to determine the optimal interface that should be designed, (b) designing the user interface [note: no matter how experienced the user interface designer, there are always usability problems with every new website or software product], (c) objectively and scientifically testing the user interface to make sure that all of the human factors heuristics have been met and that the software of the website is truly easy to use. The purpose of this book is to provide to software developers, managers, and marketing specialists a very easy, step-by-step instruction book on how to quickly and inexpensively set-up and run a Usability Testing program at your company, university, government office, or any other complex business of organization.

A company can spend truly extraordinary sums of money on the creation of a usability lab and experienced staff. It is my belief, however, that it is not necessary to spend a great deal of money in order to obtain the usability data you need to improve the ease-of-use of your website (or software, etc). Identical results can be achieved with a comparatively simple, inexpensive testing setup and moderately trained individuals. The testing equipment discussed in this book can be purchased for about $800.

The important point is that the ROI of a typical Usability Testing program must be brought to the attention of senior management and the groups responsible for budgets. Compared to almost any other investment the payback on an investment in Usability Testing is quicker and more significant. Bias and Mayhew (1994) document on pages 9 through 59 numerous case studies in which both large and small companies have seen savings from $100,000 in the first year to $6,800,000 in the first year through the implementation of human factors principles and Usability Testing. They cite numerous examples of first-year cost-benefit ratios of 1:2. The authors cite examples of internal rate of return of 26% to 27% in the first year.

Thus, for a business, incorporating a Usability Testing program is more than wanting to do something positive for the end user; it is a business model that any CFO would find compelling.

This book is designed to be used by the product development teams within a company, but will also prove useful to management. Whenever possible within this book a specific research method or point of view it tied to the potential financial gain to the company by following this point of view. The primary goal of this book is to make it so simple to conduct Usability Testing that people within all parts of the organization will appreciate the need for Usability Testing and will carry out their own tests. My approach with this book is to tell you just what you need to know to run effective Usability Tests, and to leave the theoretical discussions to another text. I hope I have achieved this simple goal.

II. Overview of Usability Testing Principles

People in product development often confuse Usability Testing with market research methods. After all, in both cases one is attempting to understand what the consumer thinks about your product and if it has the correct feature plus price combination to elicit a purchase. However, there is a very important and significant difference between the two. In the "market research" model, the consumer examines a product, and then provides his/her opinion of the product—their likes and dislikes—their preferences. It is a <u>subjective</u> evaluation. The researcher records what they <u>say</u> about their likes and dislikes regarding the product.

In "Usability Testing" the researcher does not rely solely on what the person says regarding their experience in using the product. Just like the "market research" model the consumer uses the product, and carries out "real world" problems, just as if they were using the product in an actual situation. However, the Usability Testing approach requires a somewhat different mindset. And having this particular mindset is the key to conducting successful Usability Testing. The mindset is that the researcher is not going to rely on just what the test Participant says, but the researcher is also going to objectively measure how the test Participant actually performs as they carry out these "real world" problems. That is, the researcher is going to measure the speed with which the test Participant can carry out a Task, whether or not they make errors in using the product, and whether or not they need to ask for assistance while trying to complete the "real world" problems. The important point here is that these are objective measures of the ease-of-use of the product. This is science. This approach to research yields more powerful, more defendable findings, and leads to better decisions with regard to the ways in which the product (or software) should be designed and built.

Usability Testing mindset is: focus on what the user <u>does</u> when using the product, and not so much on what they say. We want an objective measure of their <u>behavior</u>, which, in turn, is a measure of the "ease-of-use" of the software/website or other type of product. The goal is to obtain quantitative data, as opposed to just qualitative data.

The Usability approach is to get a "real-world" snapshot of the actual use of the product, to see if people will find it easy-to-use once the product or the website has been launched and is in the marketplace. If it is not easy to use, we want to find out what's wrong with it and correct it. It is much cheaper to fix a product before it has been launched than after. Furthermore, the goal is to uncover the <u>specific</u> changes that need to be made. Far too often an analysis report is delivered to management that simply says "people can't find what they need on the website". This kind of input does little good. Usability Testing identifies the specific parts of each screen or of each Task with which users are having problems. By applying the principles of human factors, one can create a design to fix the problem.

Usability Testing involves 7 steps:
(1) Look at current performance and determine where the problem lies.
(2) Conduct a Task analysis to determine how a job should optimally be performed.
(3) Create a "first draft" or a prototype of the product.
(4) Create a set of real-world Tasks that the user would typically complete when using the finished product.

(5) Set up a Usability Testing room where people can be observed and a Moderator can ask non-judgmental questions to understand how the user is thinking.

(6) Have observers measure the number of times people have difficulty or make mistakes; note where the mistakes occur. Time each Task to learn if there is a quicker way to get a job done. Count the number of mouse clicks and keystrokes, because users typically want to get a Task done in as few clicks as possible.

(7) Summarize findings from all of the data collected and based upon this scientific information, make recommendations on ways to improve the product, the website, the procedures a department follows to do billing, a new software application, and so on.

III. Definitions & Explanations

In this book I regular refer to the usability of a "website" as the product for which the user interface is being designed. However, the product could also be a piece of enterprise software, some consumer software, a medical electronics device, a speech user interface, a hand-held device, and even a process that a department uses to accomplish their routine activities. Usability Testing is appropriate for every product or service that is used by people within an organization. Also note, I use the term "product" or "software application" throughout the book—all of these terms refer to the particular user interface to which the Usability Test is being applied.

I have capitalized certain critical words in this book (such as Task, Participant, and Moderator, etc.) for emphasis.

The "user interface" refers to any aspect of the product with which the person using it comes in contact. Primarily, this is the information presented on the screen (how it is organized, its clarity, its aesthetic appearance), and the control buttons or choices available to the user (buttons or links on the screen to click on or keyboard entries). The user interface concerns the operation or functioning of a product. In this report, the user interface is sometimes abbreviated as "UI".

In market research, the focus is on a person's opinion; it is important to know a person's preference for one product over another as that is likely to be a factor in the purchase decision. In usability research, our focus is on human performance: when a person is using a product, can they operate it easily and intuitively, without any assistance from the researcher? In Usability Testing we obtain objective, measurable data on the actual use of the product. Having these data enables us to improve the design and make the product easier to use. For this reason, in market research we refer to the people in the study as "respondents", while in Usability Testing we refer to the people in the study as "Participants".

Usability data are very good predictors of product success: poor usability, the product is likely to be unsuccessful. A highly usable product has a greater chance of being successful in the marketplace. Thus, market research and Usability Testing are complimentary rather than adversarial.

There are a number of terms that are used which are similar to, and for most practical purposes, are the same as usability and Usability Testing. Some of these other terms include: "human factors engineering", "customer experience management", "ergonomics", "user-centered design", "human factors", and "user-friendly design".

CHAPTER 2

How to Determine Whether or Not Usability Testing Is Needed

Step 1: Look at the Performance Inside Your Company
There are many signals a company may receive that indicate that Usability Testing is needed. Here are but a few examples:

1. You have received complaints on your toll-free phone number, or have received numerous customer service calls from confused users;
2. Your session logs indicate that of all the customers who put something into the shopping cart, only a small percentage can successfully make it through to checkout, and thus make your cash register ring;
3. You have conducted Usability Testing or user testing and have obtained poor results;
4. Sales people within your organization have reported that customers are not happy with the ease-of-use of your product;
5. A reporter or other industry specialist has reviewed your site relative to the competition and yours has come up short;
6. A consumer panel has examined it and given it a thumbs down;
7. Marketing people within your organization find it hard to use;
8. Your gut tells you it stinks;
9. Focus group research has indicated that people dislike your site;

There are many indicators that your products or your websites are difficult to use. Whatever the indication, when you find this kind of negative information about your site or your product, do not ignore it, act upon it.

Step 2: Create a Team and Think "Consensus Building"
The power of consensus building within your company cannot be stressed enough. Get people behind your Usability Testing efforts. Poll the other groups in the organization with regard to problems or issues on the current website. As many people as possible should have the opportunity to help define the problem.

Step 3: Consider Getting Outside Help
My experience has shown that nearly every high-tech product needs usability help. The people who design and develop the overall service are normally

stretched to the limit in building the back end, and normally run out of time or resources when it comes to the user interface.

In addition, the people who have been associated with the development of the product throughout are simply too close to the product to do an objective job on the user interface. It makes sense to have a usability specialist or an outside consultant do this work.

Step 4: Create the Mindset of Quick Turnaround of Data

First, an important point: A great plus associated with the Usability Testing model is speed of getting results. The entire process in this book can be done in 3 to 4 weeks—less once the procedures are in place and people are trained. The goal of Usability Testing is to get action-oriented UI suggestions to the designers as quickly as possible in order to keep the development cycle short. This is the mindset of usability people: get useful information and get it fast.

Step 5: Perform a Competitive Analysis

A useful suggestion made by Krug (2000) is that prior to performing Usability Testing on your site you should set up and run a formal Usability Test comparing your competitiors' websites to your website. This provides some market information that may prove to be useful, and it helps you identify specific features that your competitors have that you do not have—but should have in order to "leap frog" your competitors in the marketplace. In addition, this procedure will give you practice in conducting the Usability Testing on your website. If you do not have the time or the resources to conduct a formal Usability Test of your competitor's websites, it is a good idea to set up a "roundtable" of the people with the most experience in your organization and go through your competitors' websites and identify areas in which your competitors either do a better job at making a website easier to use (they perform an identical function to your website, but do so with fewer keystrokes and mouse clicks). A second reason for doing this is to determine if your competitors have certain new features and capabilities (that your website or product does not have) that you think will be appealing to your end users. You may want to match or exceed your competitor on this feature. If you fall behind in the quest for features that improve products, you are likely going to get into trouble.

Step 6: Perform a Cost/Benefit Analysis

The above recommendations relate to product/website design and improvement. However, you are unlikely to have any success selling them to senior management without a solid analysis of the ways in which these improvements will positively impact the bottom line. Do your homework. Many controlled research studies have been conducted that clearly document the cost-justification of Usability Testing. Typically, an investment in Usability Testing pays for itself and makes a positive contribution to the bottom line within 3 to 6 months (Please see Bias & Mayhew, 1994).

<u>Checklist for Chapter 2</u>

- ☐ Let people know that Usability Testing is quick and action-oriented

- ☐ Find out if there are usability problems by: surveying users (focus groups), look at your toll-free number call-ins, look at your session-abandon rate, discuss with marketing, look at competition, talk to sales.

- ☐ Document the usability problems you have in order to make case for conducting Usability Testing

- ☐ Build consensus of people who back the Usability Testing effort.

- ☐ Conduct a cost justification analysis to determine the investment payback period.

CHAPTER 3

How to Develop the Test Plan

Step 1: Examining One Design or Testing Two Separate Products/Websites?
Before you begin you need to have a plan documenting what you want to test (specifically), what exactly are your "customers" needs, who is going to do what, make sure you have all of the needed resources, and so on. An initial decision you need to make is whether your Usability Test is a comparison between two (or three) different versions of a website or a software application (Version A vs. Version B vs. Version C—in order to see which is better), or whether your test is an evaluation of a single website or software application in order to quickly determine if it is "usable" and meets some criteria for ease-of-use as agreed upon by management.

If it is a comparative Usability Test (Version A vs. Version B, or A vs. B vs. C), you must be careful to make sure that every Participant is exposed to the two or three versions under identical circumstances. Alternatively, different groups of people can be selected to use each version you are testing. That is, the only things that should vary as the Participants are exposed to the two (or three) versions are the specific user interface design features you wish to evaluate. The versions should not be modified or adjusted in any way during the Usability Test as this will have a negative impact on the data you obtain. In addition, the order of presentation of the two (or three) versions should be counterbalanced to eliminate any effects due to order of presentation.

If it is a monadic test (evaluation of a single version), you have more leeway with regard to making modifications to the UI (in order to evaluate different design solutions) as testing progresses.

Step 2: A Quick Test or an Experiment?
A related question to be asked at the onset of a Usability Test is whether the evaluation is being done to gain quick, practical answers to help design a product or a website, or if the test is being done to prove whether one product or one user interface is significantly better than another. The latter question is often asked

when an organization is getting ready to make a significant investment in a new product, and the heads of the organization want to make sure (based upon scientific facts) that one version of a product is better than another version (will be quicker to use, will result in fewer errors, and so on). At the University of Miami we do quite a bit of work for the government and one of the purposes of our usability research is to provide scientific data to assist people in making the correct decisions with regard to the design of a new product. However, most people who conduct Usability Tests are simply trying to find out if a given design is usable and gaining information quickly is more important than carrying out a scientific experiment and conducting statistical tests. If you are conducting a quick test to determine the usability of a product, this book contains all of the guidance you will need. If you are conducting a more comprehensive scientific test this book contains much of the information you will need (see Chapter 13 on statistical tests), however, you may also want to consult one or more of the book in the Reference section on the design of experiments and the performance of statistical tests.

Step 3. Arrange for All of the Resources You Will Need

To conduct a Usability Test you will need: a fully-functional prototype of the product or website, a manager of the test, a test Moderator or researcher, an assistant or observer, a testing room and an observation room, videotaping equipment, stopwatches or other timing equipment, test Participants, a set of well-designed Tasks, money with which to compensate the Participants, and an assortment of test materials, questionnaires, and observation tally sheets. All of this needs to come together under the direction of a test manager who is experienced in Usability Testing. While this seems like an extensive list of requirements, most of the items mentioned can be obtained inexpensively and, in general, Usability Testing is not a drain on budgets and the tests can be accomplished quickly and the findings returned to the designers within a day or so. Thus, Usability Testing is an extremely practical product development tool and its ROI is dramatically appealing. And, of course, make sure you have included all of the necessary people on the team so that you may obtain the different points of view of a variety of people and everyone feels that they have part ownership of the research.

Step 4: Write a Simple Brief Document Detailing the Work that is to be Done

Even though you may have it clear in your head as to what you wish to accomplish with this research, it is a good idea to write everything down, even in quick, outline form, so that everyone on the team is clear on the objectives and each person's responsibilities. As mentioned throughout this book, you will obtain the best results when you solicit the opinions of a number of different people on the

Participant do them in the order of 1 to 9. This will create a "learning effect" and may cause the obtained data to be incorrect. Vary the order of presentation.

Step 8: Be Careful with the Specific Wording Used
Don't use words in the Task that are the same as those used on the user interface itself. This will be leading, making the Task too easy. At the same time, don't use misleading information in the wording of the Task that will make it unrealistically difficult. Use words that are neutral and do not "help" the Participant, but also do not trick the Participant.

Step 9: Pilot Test the Wording of the Tasks
Have some of your co-workers (those not familiar with the project) read through the Tasks to make sure that the wording and the activity you are asking them to do is clear.

Step 10: During the Usability Test, get a Rating after each Task
I have found it to be very useful to have the Participant quickly rate on a 1 to 10 scale (10 = Very easy and 1 = Very difficult) while the Task is fresh in their mind. You may also want to ask them their "quick gut reaction" to the Task, however, Participants sometimes will want to talk forever, and this will get the testing off track. So, get just a rating and a brief response then move on. Sample Tasks and the Rating Scales are given in the Appendix. Each Task should be given to the Participant on a separate sheet of paper. The Participant should be focused on one Task at a time—having each Task on a separate sheet prevents the Participant from looking at the other Tasks while working on a given Task.

Checklist for Chapter 4
- [ ] Determine what a user would typically do in using the website; make sure the Tasks selected simulate "real-world" situations

- [ ] In addition to "typical" Tasks, identify some difficult Tasks

- [ ] Identify the Tasks that you think might have usability problems, skip the "no brainers"; prioritize the Tasks and select the important ones

- [ ] Write the Tasks using wording that does not "give away" how to complete the Task, but at same time, do not use words that intentionally confuse; use neutral wording

- ☐ Identify the correct response for each Task; write it down for the test

- ☐ Test each Task out and make sure they work on the website

- ☐ Print each Task on a separate sheet of paper

- ☐ Generate probe questions for each Task

Chapter 5

How to Develop the User Profile—The Screener

The Screener is used to make sure that you recruit the correct Participants for your study. I had mentioned earlier that we have in our mind the "profile" of our typical end user of the product or website. The Screener is used to make sure we obtain this type of individual for the Usability Test. It is important to include people in your Usability Test who are similar in their experience level, in their areas of interest, and in their demographics as those people who will be the eventual end users of the website, the product, or the software application being developed.

For example, if you are testing a website that you know will be used mostly by Internet novices, you do not want to select people for your Usability Test who are highly experienced Internet users. Among other variables, you want to include people in your test who match the skill level of the ultimate end users of the website or the software. The Screener ensures that the appropriate people are selected for the Usability Test.

However, getting an exact demographic fit is not as critical in Usability Testing as in market research. The reason for this is that people do not vary as greatly in behavior (how they carry out tasks) as they do in their opinions.

Step 1: Use the Screener in the Appendix as a Template
In the Appendix of the book is a sample Screener and it would be a good idea for you to use it as a template as you develop your Screener. But feel free to modify it as necessary to meet the needs of your particular study. Below is a sample (but not limited to these) of some of the characteristics of the Participant that can be "screened for":
- Be the person at their company who is responsible for a certain job
- Spend at least 5 hours a week online, not including e-mail
- Having never made a purchase online
- Being between ages of 18 and 60
- Being female
- Being a customer of a certain company

- Not being a customer of a certain company
- Having a household income of at least $50,000 per year
- Owning a portable phone and a PDA
- Using a computer at least 15 hours per week
- Having at least 2 years experience with Windows software
- Being an Internet novice, or a novice computer user

Step 2: The Group Agrees Upon the Profile of the Typical End User
As with the other steps, it is important to have the different members of the team (particularly marketing) agree on the type of individuals to be used in the test. Include all of the appropriate people in designing the Screener and get sign-off before proceeding.

Step 3: Determine if you will have Outside Agency do the Recruiting
There is a temptation to simply use people within your company as the Participants for the Usability Test. This should be avoided, however, if you do not have the budget to obtain people from the general population, use whomever you can obtain; some Usability Testing is better than no Usability Testing. However, the best way (the most unbiased way) to obtain subjects is to draw a sample from the general population (however, if, for example your population of interest is "people who manage the office and do clerical work in law firms" then you would limit your recruiting to this population) is to have an outside recruiting firm do the work for you. They probably have databases of people who match your end user profiles, and you will save a great deal of time by having them make all of the phone calls, administer the Screener over the phone, and set up the appointments. There are many such agencies all over the country and you can obtain a list of the agencies in your city via the section on this topic in the Appendix.

Checklist for Chapter 5
- ☐ Determine what characteristics you want to "screen for"—determine the type of people you want to have in your test

- ☐ Create questions so that you will select people that have similar experience characteristics as the end user of your website or software

- ☐ Write the questions following the Screener templates given in the Appendix

☐ If your study involves organizing people into different groups, create the groups using the Screener

☐ Include a question to exclude people who are very familiar with market research or who work in the industry you are evaluating

CHAPTER 6

How to Develop the
Moderator's Guide and Probe Questions

Although the Usability Test session should concentrate on the Participant's performance in completing the Tasks (that is, focus on behavior), normally it is beneficial for the Moderator to "probe" (get the Participant's opinion) during the test session. This is useful because through these probe questions we can understand the "why" of their behaviors and not just have a quantitative measure of behavior. As a reminder, you must be careful to ensure that these probe questions and their discussions do not take up too much time between tasks. If this occurs, the smooth flow of the Usability Testing process becomes compromised, and this is likely to have a negative effect on your results.

Step 1: Develop a Structured Plan for Asking these Questions
Rather than have these probe questions being random and unstructured, it is a good idea to have a list of the issues you would like to probe for each Task. Create a well-designed questionnaire from which you will direct your questions and interactions with the test Participant after each task. As these probe questions are taking place, stay on topic and do not let the discussion ramble to other issues. Keep the discussion focused on the most important information that you need to obtain. Do not let the discussion slip off onto irrelevant topics. It is quite easy for this to happen since the Participant will want to, for example, describe for you another, unrelated, problem they had with the product/website two weeks earlier. As Moderator it is your job to make sure this does not happen. This list of pertinent issues is often referred to as the "Moderator's Guide". Use the Moderator's Guide to stay on topic and limit the unnecessary discussion during the test.

Step 2: Moderator's Guide should Focus on the "Whys" of Participant's Responses
The Moderator's Guide should ask about the "Whys" of the Participants actions during the test. For example, if the Participant spends a great deal of time looking for a button while completing a Task, we would ask them, "You were looking for a certain button to complete that Task?" "If so, what should that button be called, in order to make things clearer?" From this you are likely to identify a better label for that button. With all of these questions you are trying to better understand

what the user is thinking as they use your website or product so that you can adjust the design of the user interface so as to fit the way they think. You need to get inside their head so that you know how to build your UI so that it is as easy-to-use as possible. An example of a Moderator's Guide is given in the Appendix. Use it as a starting point to create the Moderator's Guide you will need to fit the specific needs of your Usability Test.

Checklist for Chapter 6

☐ Determine which issues are important enough to require probe questions; make sure you limit number of issues—make sure probes do not disrupt flow of Usability Test session

☐ Make a list of the probe questions

☐ Make sure the probes stay on topic

☐ Have the probes examine the important "Whys" of the Participant's actions

☐ Make sure all questions are short and very focused

CHAPTER 7

How to Develop the
Data Logging Form

The next step is to create a form that the research assistant (who is monitoring the Usability Test from the observation room) will use to tally certain things, such as the number of errors, the number of times the Participant needs to ask for assistance, etc. All of these things represent objective measures of the person as they are actually using your product. Keep in mind that this is different from asking people their opinion of your product—which is what one normally does in product research. By having accurate measures of the Participant's actual behavior you are best able to improve the usability of your software application, website, or product. It is necessary to have a formal data collection sheet, or performance measurement sheet, in order to gather these performance data reliably.

Step 1: Keep in Mind that the Data Logging Form (or Sheet) Keeps Track of Behavior

As a reminder, the goal of Usability Testing is to obtain objective, observation-based data. The goal is to measure behavior. We are interested in what the Participant actually does when using the website or the product. In addition we want to obtain this information in an unbiased manner—the data collection must be reliable. No matter who is collecting the data, the obtained data should be similar. To accomplish this, it is a good idea to have several training sessions before the Usability Test so that all of the people who will act as research assistants can define and agree upon what constitutes each kind of behavior on the Data Logging Form (such as an "error", "a request for assistance", and so on). This is described in Step 2. The Data Logging Form is used by the research assistant, who is normally viewing from behind the one-way mirror or from another room which is fed by close-circuit TV. The observer watches what the Participant does, and as certain behaviors occur, (an error for example) the assistant quickly makes a tally mark on the Data Logging Form. As time allows, the assistant should also write down what the Participant is doing, and, for example, at what points in completing a given Task that the Participant becomes confused. If possible the assistant should also write down why the Participant became confused. After each session, these data can be analyzed to identify problem areas with the UI. All of this information will help in improving the user interface and in making the product easier-to-use.

Step 2: Specify the Correct Steps to Complete Each Task
The first step in defining what constitutes "error" performance is to define the correct way to complete each Task. Keep in mind that there may be more than one way to complete each Task correctly. Thus, the Moderator and each of the people who are going to be the research assistants should sit down with the product or the website and walk through each Task and agree upon what represents the "correct path" to completing the path. You should do this several times for each Task so that each person who is going to be measuring behavior can ask questions and be sure they are clear on what constitutes the correct behavior to complete each Task.

Step 3: Define What Constitutes an Incorrect Action for Each Task
Hand-in-hand with Step 2 is defining what constitutes an "error". Notice on the sample Data Logging Form on the next page that we have also created the concept of an "inefficiency" and the idea of keeping track of the number of times the Participant needs to ask for assistance. The reason each of these measures is important is that they are indications of a user interface design that has problems. If the Participant gets off track, makes errors, and needs to ask for assistance during the Task, it is clear that the user interface is not as easy-to-use as it should be. However, the research assistants and the Moderator need to agree upon what constitutes an "error" or an "inefficiency". It is important that there is agreement among all of the researchers so that there is consistency in the data gathering. As an example, on websites, a good measure of a Participant having difficulties is the number of times they need to use the "Back" button. The use of the "Back" button is an indication that the person made a wrong choice, and now they need to go back and make the correct choice. The research assistants should keep track (by putting a "tally mark" in the appropriate box on the Data Logging Form) of the number of uses of the "Back" button and why it needs to be used. By noting where in the sequence of the Task it needs to be used, one can identify a problem area of the user interface.

Step 4: Define the Beginning and the End of each Task
Since the Tasks are going to be timed as another measure of the ease-of-use of the product, the Moderator and the research assistants need to agree upon the action by the Participant that constitutes the start of the Task, and the action that constitutes the end of the Task so that the assistants know when to start and when to stop the stopwatch. This is a fairly easy process. Normally there is an initial key that the

Participant presses to call up the first screen of the Task (and the stopwatch would be started at this point) and similarly when the Participant has reached a certain point in the sequence (a certain screen), this constitutes the end of the Task and the assistant stops the stopwatch. This is not a difficult process, there just needs to be agreement on these beginning and ending points so that there is consistency in this measurement.

Step 5: Design the Form for Fast Use

The Data Logging Form should be designed for very quick use by the observer—things tend to happen fast and furious during a Usability Test session and the form must be easy to use so that the observer does not miss important events. As time allows, there should be room on the form for the research assistant to write brief comments, which can be analyzed later.

Other behaviors by the Participant that may be indicative of good or poor usability include:

- Number of times they have to ask for help from the Moderator
- Number of times they go to online Help
- Number of times they refer to the user manual or quick reference card
- Number of times they use the Back button
- Number of times they make comments indicating frustration
- Number of times they get a "partial correct" for a Task

An example of a Data Logging Sheet is given on the next page. The format that is shown here was designed specifically for a given Usability Test that I was conducting—you should feel free to modify the form as necessary to meet the specific needs of your particular study. The important thing is that the results of your test be based upon the overt behavior of the Participant, and that it yields information on the critical variables of your Usability Test.

(Your company name; Name of the client company, if different; Name of the project—be specific; Names of people doing the data collection; and the date and time.)

Data Logging Sheet

Participant ID #: _____ Date: _____ Time: _____

Task # _____	Performance	Observations and Comments
Complete	☐ Correct ☐ Incorrect	
# of Assists	Tally	
# of Negative Remarks	Tally	
Partial correct?	☐ Yes	
# of Times Participant needs to use the "Back" button	Tally	
# of times an "inefficiency" occurs, as defined by the PI	Tally	
# of errors committed in the completion of the Task	Tally	

Task start trigger: _____ Task end: _____ Time to complete: _____

Ratings: Ease-of-use _____ Accuracy _____ Quality _____ Speed _____

Overall preference: _____   Overall rating: _____

(Your company name.)
(Name of the client company, if different)
(Name of the project—be specific)
(Names of people doing the data collection; date and time)

Instructions for the Data Logging Sheet

- The Data Logging Sheet documents the actual behavior of the test Participant and is therefore a very good indicator of the ease-of-use of the device being tested. Note that a separate Data Logging Sheet is completed for each Task carried out by each Participant. At the top of the sheet the Participant's secret test ID number is noted, along with the date, time, and the specific Task being observed at that time. Please note, this Data Logging Form is just a sample; yours may need to be different to fit the specific needs of your research.

- The assistant to the test Moderator observes the test Participant as he/she is completing each Task and makes a number of important behavioral measurements: (a) did the Participant complete the Task correctly (and space is provided if the observer wishes to write down any pertinent additional information), (b) the number of assists is a count of the number of times the Moderator needed to give the Participant some prompting as to how to complete a given Task—this is an indicator of ease of use. For each instance in which the Moderator provides some prompting, the assistant puts a "tick mark" or a tally mark within the box, (c) every time the Participant makes a negative remark about the use of the device the assistant puts a tally mark— this measure is an indicator of a lack of usability, (d) sometimes a Participant will get a Task partially correct—in those instances the assistant puts a tally mark in this box, (e) (note: this measure is not applicable to this particular study), (f) the assistant puts a tally mark here if the Participant gets the Task correct, but they did not complete the Task in the most efficient manner possible—this is an indicator of ease of use, (g) the assistant puts a tally mark here for each error the Participant makes in completing the Task.

- At the bottom of the sheet the assistant notes the ratings that the Participant provides for each Task. In other words, the Rating Sheets that are provided are just used for the Participant to look at—they do not indicate their rating on the sheet itself—they give their rating to the assistant who writes it down. This is the reason for not having a field for the Participant ID # on each of the rating sheets. Before the study begins the Moderator determines what actions by the Participant constitute both the beginning and end of each Task. The assistant has a stopwatch and determines the length of time it took for the Participant to complete the Task (another indicator of ease of use) and the assistant puts those time values in the appropriate fields at the bottom of the data Logging Form. Finally, the Participant is asked their overall preference between the two devices they used and the overall rating of that device.

<u>Checklist for Chapter 7</u>

☐ Determine what behavior (what actions) of the Participant is critical— what specific actions constitute successful completion of the Task

☐ Create a form that would enable an observer to determine when one of these Participant actions occurs, and then put a tally mark or a notation on a sheet

☐ Data Logging Form should be designed for very quick use by the observer

CHAPTER 8

How to Develop the Post-test Questionnaire

After conducting each Usability Test session, it is usually desirable to ask certain questions of every Participant. We want to get everyone's opinion about several given variables of the product. The post-test questionnaire accomplishes this.

These questions should focus on the key issues of the research. They are designed to dig deeper into what the person is feeling with regard to the look and feel of the website. It is a tool to probe for more of the "Whys" of the Participant's actions during the test.

It can be a written questionnaire, or it can be administered orally. Which you choose may be a function of the amount of time you have (with a written questionnaire, Participant can be taken to another room and you can then begin testing the next person—it's faster), or it may be a function of obtaining a standard set of information from everyone (which can be done more effectively with a written questionnaire). Oral questionnaires are better if you need to probe complicated issues.

Creating a really good written questionnaire is not as easy as it may seem. It is easy for the Participant to misinterpret a word or statement on your questionnaire—resulting in bad data. Run a pilot test of your questionnaire before using it.

Another important function of the questionnaire is to obtain a definitive answer when multiple versions are tested. For example, in a Usability Test when comparing versions A, B, and C, the Participants may have given approximately the same rating for all three. People often like to "sit on the fence". Yet, your goal is to determine which of the three is the best, and why. The questionnaire gets the Participant to focus on a given issue (after having experienced all three versions) and make a definitive statement as to which one is best.

Each question in the questionnaire should focus on just one issue. On each question, keep the Participant focused on a single problem. This will yield clear, interpretable data. On a given question, if you bring in related issues or problems, you will get confusing, ambiguous information. See the sample post-test questionnaire in the Appendix.

Previously I mentioned the importance of a Task analysis in user interface design. The questionnaire can relate back to the Task analysis. In the questionnaire, ask the Participants how well the user interface they just used would assist them in doing their job more quickly, or help them accomplish the tasks they need to do more efficiently. Get them to talk about this Task that they do in the real world.

Some of the usual issues covered in a post-test questionnaire include:
- The overall appearance of the screens: color, graphics, etc appealing?
- The amount of information on the screen: too much, too little?
- The terminology: clear, easy to understand?
- The icons: easy to understand?
- The buttons and controls: easy to access & operate?
- The overall navigation: easy to understand?
- The instructions: easy to follow?
- Error messages: clear and easy to understand?

Checklist for Chapter 8
- ☐ Identify and concentrate on the key issues of the research

- ☐ Determine whether you want to use a written vs. oral questionnaire

- ☐ Ask about their opinion on matters not covered in the performance section

- ☐ Draw questions from the Task analysis and keep your focus on the eventual Task that the user must complete using the product

- ☐ Get them to "get off the fence" and state which version they prefer and why

- ☐ Make sure each question focuses on just one issue

- ☐ Double check your wording so that there is no confusion as to what you mean

- ☐ Pilot test the questionnaire

☐ Make copies of the questionnaire so that you do not need to have copies made at the research facility

☐ Have an electronic copy of questionnaire at test site in case last minute changes need to be made

CHAPTER 9

How to Recruit Your Test Participants

It is important to make sure that the people you include in your Usability Test have a similar user profile to the person that is expected to be the end user of the product or website. For, example, if you are creating a website that offers a service to people who are brand new to the use of computers and the use of the Internet, you would not want to have computer experts as your participants in your Usability Test. The "expert" user group will not give you an accurate reading on the aspects of the user interface that novices find difficult to use. Thus, you should obtain the people for your test by following the material covered in Chapter 5, Developing the Screener. However, locating the correct people to be a part of your test and setting up appointments for them to be tested is no small matter. As a note, in the past the people used in research studies have been referred to as the test "subjects". However, The American Psychological Association recommends the use of the term test "participants" to refer to the people who take part in research studies. In this book, I will use the term "Participants".

You may decide that you would like to save money by doing the recruiting yourself, using the Screener you have developed. This involves making phone calls at random and administering the Screener to see if a person qualifies. This can be a time-consuming activity, and thus, many companies opt to have an outside recruiting firm find the people for your study. You may be tempted to just get some of your friends at work to be your test Participants, but this often results in invalid data. It is not good experimental methodology to simply gather some friends or colleagues and use them as Participants. It is important that the Participants be unfamiliar with the product, and they should be unaware of your objectives and the specific purposes of the research. Using people who are part of your company thus is often not a good idea. A list of potential Participants (outside of your company) can often be obtained from a customer list or other databases of people who are similar to your user profile.

31

Because of these requirements, and because recruiting can be quite time consuming, you may decide that it is best to hire a market research firm to do the recruiting for you. I normally use a recruiting firm. A short list of research firms that do recruiting is given in Appendix N. To see a complete list, see the list of five industry organizations that provide information on the research firms. Each of these industry groups provides a directory of market research firms—some are hard copy directories, some are online. Each of the individual firms that is listed as a provider of a research facility can also do recruiting for you.

The cost to have the recruiting done for you can vary from $50 to $90 per person. But get estimates for recruiting charges and any other costs or fees the firms might levy.

These market research firms recruit from their own database of people. They have a list of people who want to participate in focus groups, tests, interviews, etc. Sometimes from these lists comes the "professional respondent"—a person who participates in many research studies, and thus, provides information that is biased. Be sure to have the research facility exclude these individuals. A question can be included on the Screener to accomplish this.

The recruiting facility will send a confirmation letter to the selected Participants (if you do the recruiting, you should send confirmation letter), and they normally make two reminder phone calls—one about three days before the testing and one the day before or the day of the testing. Stay on top of them to make sure they do these things.

People participating in a Usability Test are provided with an incentive for helping with the study—cash that is given to them after the session. Depending upon the length of the sessions and the level of knowledge possessed by the Participant, the incentive can range from a low of $35 to a high of $100 (sometimes more). Make sure you use a sign-out sheet (the research facility will do this) in order to have an accurate record of who received the incentive.

Establish the Testing Schedule

Once the Usability Testing sessions begin, it can become very hectic. It is important to have a well-thought-out testing schedule that will allow you to spend enough time to thoroughly complete the testing, but minimize the number of days required, thus holding down costs.

Usability Testing is normally done during the day, roughly 9am to 6pm. UT sessions are also held in the evening to accommodate Participants' schedules.

It will vary depending upon type of product being tested, but one generally needs about an hour and a half per Usability Testing session.

Usability Testing is in-depth, probing research, and it takes time. Don't short change the time allocated to each person. You will need at least 1 hour.

Participants tend to "burn out" after about an hour and a half. After this point, Participants often respond haphazardly, just to get finished—the result is information of poor quality. Thus, an hour and 15 minutes to hour and a half is a good session length.

Don't schedule one session directly after another; there are things that need to be done in between sessions, so leave 15 minutes to half an hour between sessions.

This means that you may only be able to complete 5 sessions per day. Normally this is satisfactory, and 2 days of testing will provide you with all the usability information you need. However, if you need to need to test more Participants within the 2-day time frame, you may run usability sessions concurrently. You may also conduct 3 or 4 days of testing (see discussion on number of Participants required).

The information comes in quickly as the first few sessions are completed. Observers (the designers, the developers, marketing, management) will obtain a great deal of data with each usability session that is conducted; they will formulate new ideas as things progress. It is usually very productive to have a de-briefing session with the client during the day—about 2 pm. This is useful because the team can discuss ideas while they are fresh, and by the end of the day (7pm or later), ones mind tends not to function as well as earlier in the day.

In addition to recruiting people to fill each of the regular testing time slots, it is a good idea to recruit "floaters". A floater is someone who agrees to stay at the testing location for several hours in order to fill in a time slot if the regularly scheduled person does not show. Thus, if you have regularly scheduled sessions at 8:30am, 10:15am, and 12noon, the floater would be scheduled to be there from 8:30am to 1pm; if someone does not show for one of the three morning slots, they fill in. If they are not needed, at the end of the time period they are paid and sent home. Because of their extra time involvement, they are paid more than a regular Participant.

Tip: I normally like to have floaters scheduled, and if every regularly-scheduled respondent shows up, I add the floater to a testing session and conduct a two-person test.

Checklist for Chapter 9

- ☐ Make sure Screener will select desired people and has been double checked

- ☐ Create the testing schedule

- ☐ Make sure Participants are unfamiliar with the product

- ☐ Obtain a list of potential Participants, or

- ☐ Select a research firm to do the recruiting—see Appendix N

- ☐ Send Screener to recruiting firm

- ☐ Review Screener with recruiting firm to make sure they understand

- ☐ Have recruiting firm start the phone calls for the recruiting

- ☐ Make sure they recruit floaters

- ☐ Call recruiting firm regularly to oversee the recruiting

- ☐ They will send you spreadsheet as status report—review spreadsheet

- ☐ Make sure there are no "professional respondents" on the list

- ☐ Get a final list of the people recruited

- ☐ Have facility (or you) send a confirmation letter to the selected people

- ☐ Make sure they have directions to the testing location

- ☐ Make sure facility places reminder phone calls the day before testing

- ☐ Arrange for the incentives (cash) for the Participants (usually about $75)

CHAPTER 10

How to Arrange for an Outside Test Facility

To save money you may conduct the Usability Testing at your own place of business. You can use a conference room, a spare office, and so on. Please see the testing room set-up details in Chapter 11.

It is not necessary to utilize an outside test facility, but you may choose to do so. Some companies choose to conduct the testing at an outside research facility because they do not have any available space in their office, they want to keep the research separated from their office, or they want to have more sophisticated videotaping than they can achieve by testing in their own place of business.

There are market research facilities available all across the U.S.; most are located in the major markets. These facilities can be rented for one day or several days at a time.

I have used many such research facilities around the country and have found that the rates and the quality vary considerably. I have included a partial list of facilities in the major markets around the U.S. Please see Appendix N. For a complete list of facilities, please check with one of the research industry trade groups, which are given in Appendix L.

In addition, there are techniques you can use in order to gain the benefit of an outside facility, but avoid some of the excessive charges that they sometimes levy. This is discussed below. While I am not guaranteeing any of these facilities, I have used most of them and feel that they are above average.

All of these facilities provide: a receptionist to greet the Participants as they arrive for the test, waiting room with refreshments, a testing room equipped with a one-way mirror, an observation room so that the development team can see the testing real-time, a sound system to provide audio to the observation room, and video capability to record the sessions. The facility will also provide refreshments to the team in the observation room.

These facilities may not provide full Usability Testing video capabilities. That is, a two-camera (split screen) approach with one camera on the Participant and one showing the activity on the screen. However, as I have mentioned earlier, it is not necessary to have all of this recording capability in order to get quality usability data. If you need this capability and the facility does not have it, you can normally hire a local video specialist who will come to the facility and do this for you. The fees for this are sometimes considerable. Check prices.

The charges associated with renting a facility can creep up in a hurry. In addition to the fee for the room itself, the facility will add on fees for videotaping (particularly if there is an operator), preparation of test materials (making photocopies, etc.), any special equipment you need (such as a monitor, LCD projector, high-speed Internet, VCR, and so on), and the refreshments served to the Participants and the development team observing in the back room.

You can reduce or eliminate these charges by:
- o   Setting up your own video capabilities, as described in Chapter 8
- o   Preparing all of your questionnaires, Task Sheets, etc. yourself so that you do not need to rely on them
- o   Bringing your own LCD projector, monitor, etc.
- o   Providing minimal refreshments, soda, coffee, etc.

Following these suggestions can save you thousands, without sacrificing the quality of your research.

Whether or not you use an outside research facility, and regardless of the extent to which you have them provide these additional services, if you follow the guidelines spelled out in this monograph, you will obtain quality usability data.

Note: As mentioned in previous section, you may want to have the facility you select to do the recruiting for you.

To find the appropriate facility for you, first determine where you would like to conduct the Usability Testing. Although Usability Testing findings generally do not differ from one part of the country to another, to accommodate any existing regional differences, it is wise to conduct research in at least two different markets. Go through the list in Appendix N and select a couple of facilities. Call the facility and find out what specific capabilities they offer. Describe the needs of your research to them.

Get a written quote from each facility. The quote should spell out any extra charges or fees. Facilities provide quotes all of the time, and thus they should be able to get you a quote the same day.

Examine the proposals and make a determination as to which facility best meets your needs. To get more information about the facility, ask for the names of some of their clients and call them. If they say that they do not provide this information, move onto the next facility. Weigh all of these factors and make a decision as to the facility with the best fit.

Once a facility has been selected, stay in touch with them and make sure your project remains on the front burner for them. They have many projects at a given point in time and things can get overlooked.

If you need either dial-up or high-speed Internet connection at the facility, be sure to make this very clear to the facility and follow up on it. Typically, they have these capabilities, but since not everyone asks for them, special arrangements often need to be made. The procedures for getting this set up and running are not always clear to the staff with whom you will be dealing. Some facilities are much better than others on this. Also, some facilities have an AV or tech person on staff—it is best to work with them. But have them do a test run of your equipment the day before your test so that you can eliminate the bugs. The number of times I have experienced technical snags are too numerous to mention.

The facility will take care of paying the Participants (the "incentive") after the test session (the facility will have a sign-out procedure), but they normally require that you send them a check for the full amount of the incentives before the testing date.

Checklist for Chapter 10
- ☐ Determine the geographic market for your test

- ☐ Determine the capabilities you would like to have for your test, i.e., one-way mirror, full videotaping, small vs. large testing room, number of observers

- ☐ Determine if the facility will be doing the recruiting

☐ Go to the Appendix of this book and select a facility, or go to websites of the research industry groups shown in Appendix N and select several facilities

☐ Call each facility and get description of their facility and capabilities

☐ Ask them if they have Usability Testing capabilities, high-speed access, etc.

☐ Send them your Screener and other specs for your Usability Test

☐ Get quotes from each facility

☐ Weigh factors and select facility

CHAPTER 11

How to Set-up the Usability Testing Rooms and the Video Equipment

The basic Usability Testing set-up consists of simply a computer connected to the Internet, enough space around the Participant for the Moderator to sit, observe, and ask questions, an observation room, and videotape equipment to record the session. You can spend a great deal of money on building a Usability Testing lab with sophisticated video and sound system equipment, however, a very functional set-up can also be created on a limited budget.

It is key to be able to have some of the development team be able to observe the Usability Testing real time. If you have a testing facility with a one-way mirror, sound system, and video recording capability, fine; you may skip this section. If you do not have such an arrangement, no problem; you will still be able to conduct quality Usability Testing.

What you will need is a simple video camera (it can be an inexpensive handy cam, etc.), a microphone, about 50 feet of coaxial cable, and a TV or monitor.

Most companies have a TV handy, and some will have a video camera. If you do not have a handy cam, you can purchase a basic camera for around $400. Make sure the camera has an adapter to allow a coaxial connection to the camera—most cameras have this capability. Also, be sure to purchase a tripod for the camera.

You can purchase a desk-top microphone that connects into the video camera. They are inexpensive—less than $50. I like the PZM microphones they use the desk surface to pick up sound.

The coaxial cable (need about 50 feet) is inexpensive and can be obtained at Radio Shack, or similar store, for about $30.

Placement of Camera: See diagram on next page—Set the camera up in the room in which the Usability Testing will be conducted. Set it up in the corner of the

39

room, about 10 to 15 feet from the Participant. It should be behind and to the side of the Participant and aimed over their shoulder.

It should be directed so as to pick up a clear shot of the computer screen. Use the zoom on the video camera to get a close up of the screen—you will be able to see what is on the screen, and see the Participant moving the cursor on the screen.

At the same time, with the microphone next to the computer, you will be able to hear what the Participant is saying at the same time you see what they are doing on the screen, thus providing a complete usability picture.

Alternatively, if you'd like to get facial expressions of the Participant and their interaction with the Moderator, you can place camera to the side or facing the Participant. However, in this case you will not get a screen shot, which is generally needed for the analysis.

Most video cameras have a red LED light on the front of the camera that flashes while the camera is recording. Even though the Participant may not be looking directly at the camera, this flashing LED may be a distraction and you may want to place a piece of black tape over it.

It is very prudent to conduct a pilot test of your video set-up well before conducting your first session. Typically, there are difficulties and you may need time to run out to the electronics store for more coaxial cable, an adapter, and so on.

Checklist for Chapter 11

☐ Set up video camera on tripod in corner of room—shoot over shoulder of Participant and get close-up of screen

☐ Arrange testing table and chairs so that neither Participant nor Moderator is blocking camera

☐ Connect coaxial cable to camera and run cable into observation room—connect cable to TV

☐ Set PZM microphone on testing table—run mic cable to camera and connect

☐ Put cassette into camera

☐ Turn on camera and TV and test video and audio pick up

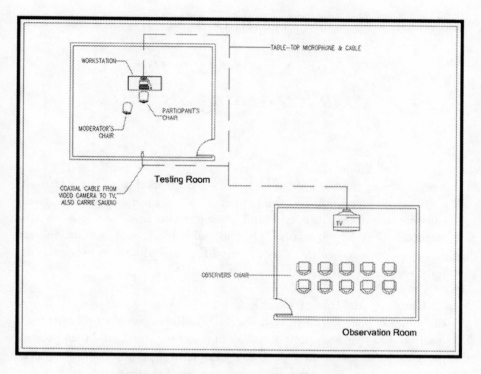

Illustration by Sam Ward, University of Miami

CHAPTER 12

How to Conduct the Usability Testing Sessions

Step 1: Conduct a Pilot Test
It is a good idea to run a couple of "dry run" participants through your Usability Test prior to conducting the real thing. This can act as a test of all your hardware and software running the prototype, and it will give you a chance to test the hand out materials (Data Logging Form, Questionnaire, Moderator's Guide, and rating Scales) to see if any of them require modifications prior to running the real Usability Test.

Step 2: Conduct Trial Run of Your Data
Prior to running your Usability Test, Dumas (1988) recommends creating some hypothetical data that you might obtain from your test. You should then perform the statistical analyses on these data that you plan on performing on your real data, and based upon this analysis, generate certain hypothetical results to your test. This exercise has two benefits: (a) it ensures that you have all of the steps, procedures, and materials ready for the test, and (b) it helps you avoid the very negative emotion one gets when you realize that the data you obtained will not answer the questions that represent the objectives of your research.

Step 3: Ensure the Moderator is Completely Neutral
Someone at your company can conduct the Usability Testing sessions; it does not have to be someone with an advanced degree in human factors engineering or user-centered design. However, the person must have good listening skills and must ask the right questions. Please see Chapter 15 for more information on this topic. However, it is critical that the Usability Testing Moderator be completely neutral and unbiased in their opinion of the user interface and the functioning of the website or product. It is very easy for the Moderator to influence the Participant's performance, and if the Moderator is not careful, they can influence the results of the study, thereby negating the value of the entire effort.

As a practical matter, a user interface design effort or a Usability Testing project nearly always has some political agenda tugging at it behind the scenes. It is critical that the Usability Testing person conducting the study separate themselves from these influences. The role of the usability person is to "go to bat" for the end user and create a product that is truly easy-to-use. If a researcher is swayed by these political forces, a less-than-optimal user interface will result.

Step 4: Establish a Comfortable, Relaxed Setting

When the Usability Testing session begins, the Moderator must establish an informal, comfortable setting for the Participant. When first greeting the Participant, the Moderator must make them feel relaxed (that they should feel comfortable giving their opinions about the product being tested). The Moderator must convey that they are accepting of anything the Participant says, but at the same time, keep an objective stance.

Step 5: Describe the Procedures

In several sentences, briefly describe what the research is about (describe it in a neutral manner) and why it is important to have them participate in the study. This initial chat needs to be informal (to put the Participant at ease), but it must also be neutral and not influence the Participant in any way.

Step 6: Hand out the Introduction & Instructions Sheet

Because consistency is required, it is a good idea to have an Introduction sheet typed up so that the Moderator can read the introduction to the Participant (this results in precise wording each time), or to closely paraphrase the introduction with each Participant. I usually type up the Introduction sheet, have a copy for the Participant, and read the Introduction out loud while the Participant follows along. The Introduction sheet should inform the Participant that they will be carrying out certain "real world" Tasks. They should complete the Tasks just as they would normally do at home or at the office.

In the introduction it is also necessary to inform the Participant that the session is being videotaped and that some of your colleagues are observing from another room.

Finally, in the introduction I like to tell the Participant that during the session I want them to "think out loud". Tell them that as they complete each Task, you would like them to tell you what's going through their mind. For example, as they are trying to complete a Task they may get stuck because they don't understand the meaning of the labels on the various buttons or controls on the screen. The control they need may, in fact, be on the screen, but, for this person, it is mislabeled. If they are thinking out loud, they would say, "I am trying to do this Task and I am looking for a key called X". This is useful information. It gives us a glimpse of how the consumer views the problem and the correct terminology to use.

A sample Introduction and Instructions sheet is presented in the Appendix.

Step 7: Explain What to Expect to the Participant

As part of the Introduction you need to let the Participant know what to expect, however, be careful not to tell them too much about how to use the product. That is, do not teach them how to use it or give them a demonstration. Be sure you do not "lead" the Participant to give the kind of answers for which you (or your client) are looking. Continue to remind yourself to be neutral and unbiased. Make it clear that this is a test of the website (or software)—it is not a test of them. This helps to put the Participant at ease. Indicate that there are no "right" or "wrong" answers—you just want them to experience the website so that they can provide their opinion of it. Indicate that this is their opportunity to have an impact on the design of a new product—this is their chance to get in their "2 cents". Tell them that the things that you learn from this will be passed on to the designers to make improvements to the website (or software). Tell them that this is important research and that their opinions will be analyzed and used. Their participation is needed to improve the ease-of-use of the website or the product. And, to abide by regulations of the IRB (Institutional Review Board) policy, tell them that if they wish to discontinue and leave the test session, they may do so at any time.

Step 8: Moderator, Keep in Mind: It's About Human Behavior

We talk about getting their <u>opinion</u>, but, of course, as usability specialists we are primarily interested in looking at their <u>performance</u> while using the product. But that is a distinction of which the Moderator should be aware, but not necessarily the Participant. We are interested in their subjective opinion, but this is in addition to the main concern of human performance.

Step 9: Arrange the Participant's and the Moderator's Seats

Where the Moderator sits relative to the Participant may be important. Sitting next to the Participant represents a more relaxed configuration and may yield more fluid conversation. However, it is important that the Moderator not send any non-verbal signals (facial expressions, etc.) to the Participant relative to their interactions with the product. Even the slightest nod of acceptance, etc. can influence the Participant's behavior, which will contaminate the data. The Moderator-Participant relationship is much like that of therapist-patient: you wish to establish a sort of stream-of-consciousness flow of thoughts, but eliminate any influences that you, as Moderator, might have. Please see Chapter 15 for a more complete discussion of this topic.

Step 10: The Participant Gets "First Impression" of the Product
Normally, before beginning the first Task, it is a good idea to have the Participant scan/review the homepage (or some start screen for the software or product). This very first impression often reveals a great deal about the Participant's <u>perception</u> as to whether or not the product is easy-to-use; and perception is important. What is their initial "gut" reaction to the look of the screen? Does it seem clear, simple? Is it clear what the site (or the product) is all about from just looking at the homepage? Does the screen seem inviting—does it make you want to use it? Are there any terms on the homepage that are unclear? It is a good idea to get these "initial reactions" before moving to the specifics of the Tasks.

Step 11. Hand Participant the First Task (it should be on a single sheet of paper)
Next, give the Participant the first Task (every Task should be on a separate sheet of paper). Tell them to carry out the Task just as if they were at home or work.

Step 12. Let the Participant Work while the Moderator Observes
Then, as Moderator, you just observe. You will have the urge to talk about the Task, to explain it, to help them get started. This is what you are not allowed to do. They must do the Task on their own, without any assistance from you. You just observe and make notes on what they do, but do not prompt or give directions.

The exception to this rule is when the Participant has attempted the Task, is stuck, and you have learned what you need to know about the UI for that Task. In this case, note your findings and move on. Do not let the Participant feel foolish or stupid.

Step 13: For Some Tasks, Leave the Room
If you have trouble pulling back from helping the Participant, you may want to leave the testing room and follow their progress from the observation room. I do this in some studies and it forces the Participant to work on their own. Or, you may want to sit behind the Participant. Also, for some Tasks, you can obtain a different kind of information if you are not in the room. Try it. Where ever the Moderator sits, the Moderator and the assistant should write down their observations of what the Participant is doing, where they are making errors, and so on. The assistant should be filling out the Data Logging Form.

Step 14: Have Participant Complete Rating Scale for that Task
Right after the Participant has completed the Task, put the Rating Scale(s) in front of the Participant and ask them how they would rate the task on "ease of completing task" (or what ever variable the Rating Scale is measuring).

Step 15: Have a Very Brief Probe Session
Right after they have provided their rating, you should probe: "What was your reaction to that Task?" Get their spontaneous thoughts and remarks. Probe for the "Whys" of their performance on the Task. "Why did you click on Button X rather than Button Y?" "Explain why you used the Back button." And so on. Get them to talk about what's going through their head. When you hear the same thing from a number of Participants, you will have zeroed in on a usability problem. Systematically keep track of these findings. Although the Participant may want to talk at length about their reaction, the Moderator needs to have the skill to bring the discussion to a close once the important information has been obtained, without giving the impression that you are cutting off the Participant, and thereby getting them to act defensively.

Step 16: Give the Participant the next Task Sheet
After you have completed the probe questions for Task 1, give the Participant the next Task and repeat the process.

Step 17: Have Quick Debriefing Sessions
The information comes in very quickly in the first few sessions. Initially, the Moderator and any other members of the research team who are observing soaks up a great deal of information. It is a good idea after the first two or three Participants to have a de-briefing session to determine what everyone has learned and if there are any other issues that need to be covered in the Usability Test. It is useful for the team to discuss ideas while they are fresh in their minds and perhaps suggest needed modifications to the UI or to the test procedures. A regular question that many clients ask whether or not it is Ok to make modifications to the product or the user interface of the website in the middle of a Usability Testing program. In controlled psychological experiments this is not acceptable. By changing the independent variables while testing is in progress will contaminate the data. However, in Usability Testing, where the goal is to gain as much practical knowledge as possible in a very limited amount of time, making such changes is acceptable. The only caveat to this is to keep very accurate, systematic records of all findings obtained with one version of the product or website before making a change to the UI being tested. It is easy to confuse the new version of

the user interface with the earlier version if you have not been diligent about your research notes.

Step 18: Administer Post-Test Questionnaire
After the Participant has completed all of the Tasks and you have had your final probe session, you would like to get the Participant to look back on all of the Tasks that he or she completed and get them to summarize the things that they found difficult to use with any of the products/websites you showed them. If the test was an A vs. B comparison test, get them to decide which of the two they felt was easiest to use. There is a tendency in a wrap-up session to get a great deal of "middle-of-the-road" comments, and the Participant will tend to do some "sitting on the fence" with regard to their overall opinions. It is the job of the Moderator to probe and ask questions to get them to commit to an overall preference. The design of the Post-test Questionnaire should reflect this. At this time you would hand the Post-Test Questionnaire to the Participant and they would complete it. You may prefer to give a copy of the questionnaire to the Participant, but then you, the Moderator, asks the questions and fills in their answers. But note, this information represents the Participant's subjective reaction to the ease-of-use of the product and this should be secondary to the analysis of the performance data.

Step 19: Check to See if there are any Additional Questions from Research Team
In most Usability Testing settings there will be other members observing the test session from another room either through a two-way mirror or via closed-circuit TV. It is a good idea at this point to go into the other room and see if any of the observers (some of whom may be from upper management) have any questions. During the Usability Test session the observers may see things that the Moderator misses. The observers' probe questions are sometimes helpful in uncovering more information. In addition, if someone from upper management feels that a certain question should be covered in the test but has not yet been asked, it is a good idea to get that topic area covered.

Step 20: Two-person Usability Testing
The discussion up to now has focused on testing one person at a time. However, there are some benefits to be had by testing two people at once within a structured Usability Testing session. In this situation, two people, who do not know each other, sit down at the terminal and are given Tasks to complete, just as with regular UT. But they are told to work on the Task together. They are told that the Moderator will not help them, and they are told to imagine that they are at home or at work and need to solve this problem (the Task). The Moderator may leave the room, or they may stay and observe from inside the test room.

The benefit of two-person Usability Testing is that as the two people are completing the Tasks, they talk with each other about what they are thinking. It gives additional insight into their perceptions and their thought processes of the website or the product. You will learn things that you may not have learned from the single-person testing. The two people may say things to each other that they may not say to the Moderator.

Notes:
In addition to the video equipment described in Chapter 8, the following is a checklist of supplies and materials that you will need for your Usability Testing sessions:

- Computer workstation with connection to Internet
- Browser software similar to that which will be available to end user
- Quite room with no distractions, adequate lighting and comfortable temperature
- Data Logging Sheets
- Digital stopwatch
- Pads of paper and pens, Clipboards
- Refreshments for Participant and observers

Checklist for Chapter 12

- ☐ Assume a neutral mindset—you are not going to have any "leading" reaction to what Participant does or says—you are going to be accepting of everything he/she says—your goal is to create atmosphere in which person uses website as they would in real world, and will open up to you regarding their reactions

- ☐ Greet Participant, create informal setting; take them to test room

- ☐ Give them the Introduction sheet—questions?

- ☐ Obtain any necessary info prior to starting test

- ☐ Give them first Task—wait and observe

- ☐ Use Data Logging Sheet to record Participant's performance

- ☐ When want specific info, probe: "What's your reaction to this screen?"

☐ Be careful and make sure that you do not ask "leading" questions

☐ At end of Task, can ask 1 or 2 questions for elucidation, but do not get sidetracked; keep flow of Usability Test moving swiftly

☐ Repeat for the next Task, and continue through all Tasks

☐ On any Task, if Participant gets stuck, ask questions to understand why they got stuck, and once have this info, move on. Do not let Participant struggle and feel awkward

☐ Conduct some 2-person test sessions to obtain that perspective

☐ At end of all Tasks, administer the debriefing questionnaire

☐ At end of test, escort Participant to receptionist who will sign them out and give them their incentive

CHAPTER 13

How to Perform the Necessary Statistical Tests

The majority of researchers and human factors specialists who perform Usability Testing do not perform statistical tests on the obtained data. Usability Testing grew out of the field of experimental psychology, but one of the virtues of Usability Testing is that the tests are done quickly, very few subjects are used, and conclusions are drawn from simply noting where the problems occur and then developing design improvements. In one sense, it was never meant that Usability Testing data would be subjected to the usual tests of statistical significance. It was generally felt that very practical decisions would be made from this kind of test and that the scientific approach of statistical tests was not called for.

However, when conducting research for the government or for the Department of Defense, as is the case at the University of Miami, requirements are spelled out that the findings of this kind of research will only be accepted if rigorous, scientific statistical tests are applied to the obtained data. Critical decisions ride on the outcomes of this research and extra attention is paid to statistics.

Performing Statistical Tests on Usability Data
This is an example of how statistical tests can be applied to the data obtained from a Usability Test. By using the statistical tests, one can determine if the difference between two different user interfaces is statistically significant. Many human factors specialists do not subject their Usability Testing data to statistical tests, however, through the use of statistical tests one can be more assured of their decisions.

Let's envision that there is a software application that enables a person to quantify a production run at a factory that makes bicycles. It is critical that the user be able to quickly fill out the five screens of this application. The shift Foreman determines how efficiently a given production line is running, and then uses these five screens and enters various production data in order to optimize the production line.

By entering data such as, the number of bicycles coming off the production line in an eight hour shift, the amount of waste that is occurring, or whether or not the necessary components for a given station on the production line are delivered to that station at the time they are needed, and so on.

One can envision that there are numerous critical variables of this sort that need to be evaluated to make sure that the bicycle factory is running efficiently.

As it turns out, some IT people from within the company have created a software application to do this. Let's call this version day. And at the same time, senior management hired an outside software development shop to build an application to do the exact same thing, let's call this version be.

The companies CEO does not know which version to use, but key/she does know that speed of getting the necessary information into the system is critical and less the CEO wants to select the version that will allow the four person in the factory to get the necessary data into the application as quickly as possible. So that if changes are needed to the production line to improve productivity, this can be done as soon as possible in order to reduce waste and improve the companies. However, the decision as to which product should be purchased is a critical one since the software application costs $352,000. Thus, before making the decision the CEO wants as much scientific data as possible.

You are the usability/human factors expert in this company and the CEO has asked you to conduct a Usability Test of both versions in order to make a scientific determination as to which one is better. By better, we mean the speed of entering the necessary data.

You first create a series of 14 individual Tasks that are representative of the types of data that would need to be entered in using this application. You will have your test Participants perform the exact same 14 Tasks on both version a and version be. Your measure of the performance of each version is the total time it takes to input the data for these 25 Tasks using both version day and version be.

Let's say you select 15 for persons to participate in the Usability Test, and you have decided to use a within Participants design. That is, each person will use both version A and version B, but the order in which they use them will be counterbalanced. Your design for your Usability Test would look like this:

Version A	Order of Use		Version B	Order of Use
Participant #1	First		Participant #1	Second
Participant #2	Second		Participant #2	First
Participant #3	First		Participant #3	Second
Participant #4	Second		Participant #4	First
Participant #5	First		Participant #5	Second
Participant #6	Second		Participant #6	First
Participant #7	First		Participant #7	Second
Participant #8	Second		Participant #8	First
Participant #9	First		Participant #9	Second
Participant #10	Second		Participant #10	First
Participant #11	First		Participant #11	Second
Participant #12	Second		Participant #12	First
Participant #13	First		Participant #13	Second
Participant #14	Second		Participant #14	First
Participant #15	First		Participant #15	Second

Let's assume that we have obtained the following (hypothetical) data after doing the Usability Test to compare the two software applications under consideration. The data below = the average time (in seconds) to complete all of the Tasks for each test Participant. To determine if the difference in speed (in using the two software applications) is significantly different, we are going to perform a t-Test for repeated measures. The example below spells out the exact steps one would follow in order to execute the necessary statistical test for this particular Usability Testing problem.

First Round Version A	Time to complete (seconds)		First Round Version B	Time to complete (seconds)
Participant #1	171		Participant #1	152
Participant #2	162		Participant #2	169
Participant #3	185		Participant #3	147
Participant #4	192		Participant #4	174
Participant #5	171		Participant #5	178
Participant #6	208		Participant #6	181
Participant #7	171		Participant #7	179
Participant #8	191		Participant #8	180
Participant #9	169		Participant #9	172
Participant #10	180		Participant #10	168
Participant #11	190		Participant #11	180
Participant #12	179		Participant #12	184
Participant #13	191		Participant #13	156
Participant #14	220		Participant #14	201
Participant #15	215		Participant #15	198
Total	2,795			2,619

One could look at this result and see that Version B was quicker to use, however, we might ask is this difference statistically significant. If the company is getting ready to invest $352,000, one would want to know that if Version B was selected, the decision was scientifically based.

To analyze these data it would be best to use a t-Test for repeated measures. There are 15 steps involved in carrying out this t-Test.

1. Create a column next to the two columns of scores and calculate the difference ("D") in the scores between Version A and Version B.

2. Create a column next to that and square this difference score ("D^2")

3. Add up the column the D column

4. Add up the D^2 column.

5. Take the sum of column D and divide it by the number of people who participated in the Usability Test (N). We will call this result (i).

6. Take the sum of column D, square it, and then divide that value by N. We will call this result (ii).

7. Take the sum of the D^2 column; from this value subtract (ii). We'll call this result (iii)

8. Multiply N by (N-1). We will recall this result (iv).

9. Divide result (iii) by result (iv). We will call this result (v).

10. Take the square root of result (v). We'll call this result (vi).

11. Divide result (i) by result (vi). We'll call this result (vii).

12. The resulting value is the t-value for the test just conducted.

13. Go to the table for the Cutoff Scores for the t Distribution, which is given at the end of this section.

14. Select the degrees of freedom (df) row that is appropriate for your study, which is the number of people tested, minus 1, and look down the column that is headed by the probability value of ".05", for a two-tailed t-Test.

15. If the t value you obtained from your calculations is <u>greater than</u> the t-value that is shown in the table for your degrees of freedom and a probability value of ".05", then your statistical test is significant. That is, there is a real difference between to two groups you are testing. Alternatively, if the t value you obtained from your calculations is <u>less than</u> the t-value that is shown in the table for your degrees of freedom and a probability value of ".05", then your statistical test is not significant. That is, there is no real difference between to two groups you are testing.

Given below is the solution to the problem and a determination as to whether Version A is better than Version B, or vice versa.

P#	Version A time	Version B time	D	D^2
1	171	152	19	361
2	162	169	- 7	49
3	185	147	38	1,444
4	192	174	18	324
5	171	178	- 7	49
6	208	181	27	729
7	171	179	- 8	64
8	191	180	11	121
9	169	172	- 3	9
10	180	168	12	144
11	190	180	10	100
12	179	184	- 5	25
13	191	156	35	1,225
14	220	201	19	361
15	215	198	17	289
Sum	2,795	2,619	176	5,294

From the steps outlined above, the following calculations would be made:

Sum of column D divided by 15:   (i)   11.733

Column D, square it, then divide by 15:   (ii)   2,065.067

Take sum of D^2 column (5,294), and subtract (ii)   (iii)   3,228.933

Multiply (N) x (N-1), 15 x 14   (iv)   210

Divide (iii) by (iv)   (v)   15.376

Take the square root of (v)   (vi)   3.921

Divide (i) by (vi)   (vii)   2.992

We look in the table for cutoff scores for the t Distribution, available in the back of any statistics textbook, and with a degrees of freedom (df) of 14 (15-1), and a probability value of .05 for a two-tailed test, we see that the critical value for *t* is: 2.145.

The value we obtained (vii) was: 2.992.

Since 2.992 is greater than 2.145, we can state that there is a statistically significant difference between Version A and Version B, and that Version B is the better product. We can say that we are confident at the 95% level of confidence that the difference between the two versions, and the fact that Version B is better, is due to some inherent positive characteristic of Version B, and that there is only a 5% chance that the obtained statistically significant result was due to chance or some other random or irrelevant factors.

If you have more than two groups, you will want to use an analysis of variance (ANOVA) statistical test. Consult a statistical textbook to get information on performing an AVOVA.

CHAPTER 14

How to Present Results for Maximum Impact

Step 1: Analyze Data and Compile it into Small Modules
While the needs of managers vary from company to company, universally I have found that managers want to see a very succinct, very brief report on the findings of a Usability Testing project. People do not have time for a long-winded report.

I recommend using a "Power Point-type" summary for the report. Use bullet points. Highlight the key points so that the reader does not have to search for the important findings. Keep it simple. See Appendix I for an example of an executive summary from a Usability Testing findings report.

Step 2: Prioritize
Another "must" in the presentation of the findings is to prioritize. All Usability Tests will uncover numerous small points and details with regard to the design of the user interface, but these issues may be unrelated to the most important questions that were posed at the outset of the research—the objectives and goals of the study. Make sure you have the findings pertaining to the most important issues presented first. There are always limited resources and no development team is going to be able to address all of the potential problem areas uncovered in a Usability Test. So highlight the most important ones and make sure there are resources to fix the items that represent the most serious issues.

Step 3: Emphasize the Objective vs. Subjective Data
You will have two types of findings: Objective data-Those based upon actual observed performance by the Participants, and Subjective data-People's opinions and preferences. Keep these findings distinct from one another. Make it clear that the objective findings are based on the measurement of actual performance, and that they are likely to be the better indicator of the ease-of-use of the product. That is, the human performance data are likely to be more accurate in predicting how the product will do once it is launched. However, the two types of measurement should be fairly highly correlated.

Use graphs and tables whenever possible. Minimize the amount of text and show the main effects you have obtained through the use of bar charts, graphs, and pictures. In addition, while some of management may have a cursory understanding of Usability Testing, most will have had little exposure to it and they are likely to lump it into the same category as focus group research. This is a problem because generally Usability Testing is much more powerful in identifying ease-of-use problems. Thus, it is often good to show 10 or 15 minutes of selected video clips that illustrate exactly what Usability Testing is and gives management a glimpse of a typical end user struggling to be able to use their product—a new product into which, perhaps, millions of dollars have been invested. This becomes a powerful statement that cannot be conveyed in the text of the report. The final part of the report should be a concise list of the things that need to be fixed and which individuals on the development team are responsible for each item on the list.

Some Sample Data

Here is a sample set of findings from a study on the usability of a search engine. Shown are the performance findings of six different Tasks, along with the subjective ease-of-use ratings given to each Task.

Task #	Performance Ave. # of Errors	Performance Ave. Time to Complete		Opinion Ave. Ease of Use Rating (1 to 10 scale)
1	0.9	1 min. 43 sec.		9.2
2	2.5	2 min. 17 sec.		8.1
3	5.8	4 min. 51 sec.		4.3
4	2.3	2 min. 35 sec.		6.5
5	2.4	2 min. 19 sec.		7.8
6	1.5	3 min. 10 sec.		7.1

These data clearly revealed that Task #3 was the biggest problem. People had trouble understanding how to complete this Task. It had the highest error rate (5.8 errors), it took the longest (on average) to complete this Task (4' 51"), and it had the lowest subjective rating (4.3 out of 10). This information told us that the user interface for this Task needs to be redesigned to eliminate the problems. These data can be graphed in order to quickly identify the problem Task.

Another example involves a comparison across a number of different search engine products. The purpose of the test was to determine which search engine is best. This table shows the averages across all Tasks for 7 different search engines (the data have been adjusted for confidentiality reasons, but principle is the same). Note that there are performance data as well as opinion data

Search Engine	Performance Ave. # of Errors		Opinion Average Ease of Use Rating
Zip2	1.1		8.4
Yahoo Yellow Pages	3.2		7.1
Infospace	4.1		6.9
BellSouth	1.9		8.1
AtHand	4.8		4.8
Superpages	3.1		6.2
US West Dex	2.5		7.3

From these data it is clear that Zip2 provided the best user interface—It had, on average, the fewest errors (1.1) and the highest opinion rating (8.4). The BellSouth search engine had the next best performance.

Based upon these results, the researcher drills down into what people said and what can be seen from the videotapes to determine the specific aspect of the UI that caused the problem—then generate a design solution that solves these problems.

Stating the findings of a Usability Test (as we have just done) and determining exactly how the user interface should be re-designed to correct the problem are two very different things. While someone inexperienced in usability may be able to carry out the research and analyze the findings, you may need a usability specialist to interpret the results and formulate specific UI design changes that address the issues raised in the research.

Checklist for Chapter 14

- ☐ Calculate the performance data

- ☐ Tally the opinion data—Differentiate these data in the report

- ☐ Determine best format for very simple presentation of the data

- ☐ Use graphs and tables for clear delivery of the information

- ☐ Provide a brief explanation as to the meaning of each data point

- ☐ At end of the section, provide discussion on the specific UI design changes that should be made based upon the hard facts of the research

CHAPTER 15

How to Act On the Results:
Making User Interface Design Changes

Conducting the Usability Testing is only half the battle. All of the findings of the research are useless if you cannot get management and the design group to act upon the findings. This process becomes easier if all members of the development team have been involved from the beginning in the planning and execution of the usability work. The first phase of this chapter is to build a group that can work together well, and the second part is to draw upon, and creatively apply the principles of human factors and user interface design.

If all people have been included from the start this initial step becomes easy. If everyone has not been involved from the start some effort will be required to draw everyone into the process of re-designing the product based upon the findings of the Usability Testing. One way to do this is to get senior management involved in the project as much as possible. If your usability work is truly improving the product or system, you should not have difficulty in convincing senior management to attend a few meetings or at least indicate their support.

One way to draw certain critical individuals into the process is by making sure that each group participating in the usability evaluation program feels that they have a piece of ownership in the program and that they will receive some of the credit when management discovers that a better, more user-friendly product has been created as a result of this program. This will flow naturally if the other groups have been involved in the process from the very beginning.

The things you learn from the testing must be translated into specific user interface (UI) design enhancements. This will happen more quickly if the software development team and the engineers have been involved since the onset of the project and were available to observe the Usability Testing real-time.

As the person championing the usability cause within your company, there may be a number of forces working against you. In some cases Usability Testing is done solely for political reasons. Someone may feel that it looks good to have a usability analysis performed, but do not want to be the person responsible for pushing the change through. Change is often difficult and many people are afraid of failure.

You need to overcome this resistance. Document the cost savings associated with good usability. Illustrate how the usability enhancements will benefit the company, and the careers of those within the company. Provide a clear roadmap as to how the changes will be made, and that it is likely to require minimal resources and time to implement.

To illustrate that there is a problem, it is often useful to make a 15-minute highlight video clip from the Usability Testing sessions showing the problems that people are having in using the current version of the software, or website, etc.

Normally, if management and the development team observed some of the sessions real-time, there is an acute understanding of the need for usability and the importance of your mission. If not, you need to be able to make your case and make sure that action is taken.

You should take a leadership role in getting the modifications made. You may be able to assume the role of un-biased third party in the design effort, which will be useful in getting things accomplished.

While everyone on the team may be focused on the report itself, I think it is useful to get beyond the report and examine potential screen design changes. This helps makes things real. Let the team know that you are willing to roll up your sleeves and get your hands dirty in re-designing the UI. Have "white board" sessions in which UI changes are put up on the board, dissected, discussed, and evaluated. Structure the work sessions such that everyone can get in their "two-cents" and be part of the re-design.

Take small steps. Evaluate a portion of the UI, reach agreement on a solution, get sign-off from everyone, then move onto the next UI component.

There are numerous UI design guideline books to assist with making the specific design changes. Please see the Reference section in the Appendix. Utilize these resources as necessary to have the most productive work sessions.

Document very precisely every decision that is made during the work sessions. It is very easy to get confused as to what design changes have been examined and which ones have received final approval from everyone. So get organized and keep records of every decision made and be thorough in taking meeting minutes. Have someone be the record keeper and document all of the details of the "white board" sessions. Design-by-committee is sometimes very difficult and often results in a less-than-optimal UI. You have to make sure that intelligent (with regard to usability) decisions are made.

In the end, you, as the usability champion, should prepare a UI document that specifies all of the changes agreed upon by the team. This is the basis by which the developers will create the new UI. Specify to very precise levels in order to avoid ambiguity and an incorrect user interface.

After all of this is done, remain in the loop to answer questions and help make UI design trade-off decisions as they arise. The person running the Usability Testing often delivers their report, then is on to something else. Follow-through is important.

Checklist for Chapter 15
- ☐ Get management and development team together to review the report

- ☐ Create videotape of highlights of the testing so that people are clear as to the problems with the current UI

- ☐ Use the UI redesign as a rallying point for the group, not as wedge between members of the team

- ☐ Take a leadership role in the synthesis of new UI based upon the test results

- ☐ Get beyond the report—Get potential UI design solutions up on a white board and let everyone analyze and discuss

- ☐ Take small steps in the redesign—Work on a section, reach agreement and sign-off by all members, document, then move on

- ☐ Use a UI design guidelines book as necessary to help the team reach a solution—If necessary, step in and make a decision on design of the UI

- ☐ Precisely document all agreed-upon changes

☐ Write summary document specifying all UI design enhancements

☐ Follow-up. Work with designers and developers. Stay in the loop to answer questions and make decisions as UI design progresses

CHAPTER 16
Training the Usability Testing Moderator

Step 1: Designate Your UT Moderators
If you decide to conduct your Usability Testing program in house, it is a good idea to get two or three people who become trained in the skills of conducting Usability Tests. One important part of this is that they all receive the same training and agree upon the same methods and metrics so that there is consistency in the way you carry out your Usability Tests, and hence your findings.

Being a good UT Moderator is part science, part art. Anyone with good people skills can do it—providing he/she keeps certain principles in mind and follows the instructions I have outlined below.

Step 2: Using an Outside Moderator
If you do not feel that you have the resources in-house, of if you feel that anyone you select to be Moderator will have a bias as they conduct the research, you would be well advised to hire an outside consultant to assist you. The cost of an outside Moderator should be in the range of $900-$1,200 per day, depending upon the extent to which they help you design the study, and design the Tasks, etc., vs. simply providing moderating services during the Usability Test sessions.

Step 3: Check Them Out
If you do use an outside Moderator, check out their credentials and call at least two references or companies who have used this person's services. There are a number of well-intentioned, but unqualified people working in the usability field.

Step 4: Include Person from the Onset
The person that you hire should be included in your meetings as early as possible so that he/she is completely familiar with the specific needs and specific objectives of your study. State these needs and objectives in behavioral terms or in performance-based terms so that a determination can be made subsequently as to whether or not the objectives were met. This outside Moderator must be completely familiar with the Task sheet and be knowledgeable on the types of Task performance and responses that are likely to be obtained from the test Participants.

Step 5: You Decide to use an "Inside" Person as Moderator

If you decide to have one of the people within your company be the Moderator, this is fine—just make sure they meet certain qualifications and that they follow the guidelines stipulated below.

Step 6: Establish a Relaxed Environment

As the Usability Test Moderator it is essential that you create an atmosphere in which the test Participant is completely relaxed, trusts you, and is ready to give you his/her candid opinion about the product or website you are testing. You need to establish an atmosphere in which the test Participant can pretend they are at home or at the office and that they feel they are using the product in a "real-world" situation. Also, the notion must be reinforced that this is not a test of them, but rather, is an evaluation of the website, the software application, or the product to determine if there are certain improvements that should be made before the release of the product.

Step 7: Meet Informally before the Test Session

One way to do this is to begin informal conversations (but do not reveal the subject matter that is part of the Usability Test) with the test Participants before they are brought into the testing room. Typically, the Moderator goes to a waiting room to get the Participant to take them to the test room. As you greet them, tell them informally what they will be doing and the nature of the product that is being evaluated (but do not provide any leading information that may influence them in the test). Or ask them if they had difficulty getting to the test location, etc. Have a conversation that lets them know that you (the Moderator) are a real human being and that you want this important research session to be a successful experience for them. At the same time, the atmosphere you are creating should not be so informal that they do not take the research seriously, or that they do not take you seriously.

Step 8: You Must Not be Judgmental

Most important thing to remember in carrying out the Usability Test session is to accept everything the Participant does or says, without showing your opinion regarding their actions or comments. Don't react with surprise if they do or say something that is unexpected, amusing, or demonstrates their lack of knowledge of the content being tested. This may influence how they use the product or what they say about the product. In a way, the Moderator in a Usability Test is somewhat like a psychotherapist. You must listen to what the Participant says and observe what the Participant does without judging them in any way. At this time the assistant who is observing is keeping a tally sheet (the Data Logging Form) to record all of the actions they are taking. There is a notion within psychology that one cannot measure something without influencing the thing that they are measuring. This is likely to be true, however, by following the techniques I have just mentioned the amount of this unintended influence will be minimized.

Step 9: You May Not Show the Participant How to Use the Product

During the session the Participant will most surely reach a spot where they are not sure what to do and they will turn to you and say something like, "Is this what you want me to do"? This is a natural thing. In most situations in which one person does not know how a product works it is commonplace that the other person demonstrates how the product works. This is not the way Usability Testing sessions are conducted. The test Participant is likely to ask you (the Moderator), "Ok, what should I do next"? It is very hard for the first-time Moderator to refrain from simply answering the question (because you would like to help a person in need), however, you must not answer their questions regarding the use of the product. The rule of being a Moderator is: [Every time the test Participant asks you a question, you turn the question around and ask them what they think they should do in this situation. Right at this point it is crucial for you to "get inside their head" and understand what they are thinking (about this particular user interface question sitting before them) so that you can make improvements to the design of the user interface. After all, with a good user interface, at each point where the end user needs to decide what to do next, the user interface should clearly present the available choices and not leave the user "stranded". If the UI does not do this, it is not a very good UI. Gaining a thorough understanding of why they are not sure what to do next will guide you as you work to design a better user interface. However, this principle of not telling the Participant what to do should apply for about 15 to 20 seconds. If the Participant tries to get you to show them what to do and you say "what do you think you should do", you let them express their opinion for about 15 to 20 seconds and if they have no idea what to do, you make this note on your Data Logging Form, then you tell the Participant the correct answer, and move on. You do not want the Participant to feel incompetent and thus become nervous. Thus, you simply note where the problem occurred, casually tell them the correct answer and move on. You have obtained the information you need (the point where the problem exists in the user interface), so just move on and continue to make the Participant feel relaxed.

Step 10: Do Not Express Your Opinions about the Product

A very natural thing for people to do is to express their opinions about the product or the website—things they like and do not like about it, and so on. As a Moderator, you must suppress the urge to do this. You will influence the test

Participant and contaminate the data. The Usability Test is all about the Participant's opinions and their ability to complete the specified Task, and thus it is essential that you keep your opinions out of the discussions you are having with the Participant.

Step 11: Do Not Ask Leading Questions

In certain instances the Moderator has been working with the new product or website and cannot help but have their own opinions as to what they like and don't like about the product. There is a tendency to let ones own opinions of the product creep into the questions that are asked of the Participant. Make sure, as Moderator, that you do not ask leading questions. By leading questions I mean questions in which one point of view clearly appears to be favored, simply by the way you ask the question. For example, if you are trying to solicit their opinion on the density of information on a given web page (generally, too much information on a page makes a website difficult to use), you would not phrase your question, "Were you bothered by the large amount of information presented on this page?" This is going to bias the Participant and increase the probability that they will say that the web page contains too much information. A better way to phrase the question would be, "What was your reaction to the appearance of this web page?"

Make sure that the way that you feel about a given user interface design does not influence the way you ask your questions. For example, if comparing the presentation of information on Version A vs. Version B, don't say, "Did you like the orderly way that the results were presented on version B?" This shows that the Moderator may have a preference for B over A, and this bias is coming through in their questions. Keep it neutral, "What did you think about the way the results are presented on Version B?"

Step 12: Whenever Participant asks a Question, Turn it around and Give it Back

Very often while the Participant is carrying out a Task they will turn to the Moderator and ask, "Ok, what do you want me to do next"? Or, if you are testing a banking website the Participant may ask you "Is this percentage shown here the interest rate I would get on a 3-year CD"? (assuming that was the Task). There will be an over powering feeling to help the Participant out and give them the answer. As Moderator, you must avoid answering such questions. When the Participant asks such questions, it indicates that there is something that is not clear about the information that is presented and it is preventing them from completing the Task correctly. It is critical at this point to find out what the Participant is thinking and why the information is unclear, and why they are unsure what they should do next. A general rule is that the Moderator should not answer questions, just ask questions. Thus, in the above example, the Moderator should turn the question around and ask, "What is it that you see on the screen that indicates to you that this is the interest rate on a 3-year CD"? "What information about CD rates is not clear"? "What additional information would you like to see that would clarify this situation"? In the first example when the Participant asks, "Ok, what do you want me to do next", you should turn it around and say, "Well, in order to complete the Task, what do you think you would do next"? When the Participant is not sure what to do next in order to complete a Task, it is an indication that the information that is being presented is not clear enough. Thus, you want to dig down into the Participant's thought processes and find out what particular piece of information is causing the problem. Once you know this you can change the information that is presented and, hopefully, make it crystal clear what the person is to do next to successfully complete the task. By analyzing and solving problems in this manner you will most definitely improve the ease-of-use of your product or website.

This advice on not answering the Participant's questions (but turning the question around and asking it back to the Participant) has limits. If you have re-asked the question in a different manner and the participant is still unclear as to what they should do, simply make a note of where the problem occurred (so that you can eventually fix it), give the participant the information they need to get their question answered (so that they don't feel frustrated and begin to resent the Moderator), and then move onto the next Task. You do not want the participant to feel stupid or inadequate and have them struggle unnecessarily with a problem. You will have obtained the information you need (where is the usability problem), and now you should just move on to the next Task.

Chapter 17
Online Usability Testing

Traditional, one-on-one, Moderator-based Usability Testing is but one way to obtain usability data. Another, new methodology for evaluating the usability of your website (and this technique is generally limited to websites and software programs that can be accessed via the Internet), is online Usability Testing. This is a self-administered, web-based, automated data gathering technique.

People visiting a website are given the option of participating in the usability research. If they choose to participate, a window is presented on the left-hand side of their screen (with the main part of the site still showing on their screen).

In this left panel they are given the Tasks to complete, and as they begin carrying out the Tasks all keystrokes and clicks are recorded. Usability problems can be inferred from the clicks/keystrokes as well as from the durations of the session.

Some of the companies providing online Usability Testing include:

RelevantView	relevantview.com
Keynote	keynote.com
ComScore	comScore.com
TeaLeaf	tealeaf.com

These programs may be able to obtain the same or similar information as traditional Usability Testing, in less time and at a lower cost. In addition, because some of the packages are used remotely, a wide range of users and a large number of users can be quickly sampled.

Generally speaking, these online Usability Testing programs are a good resource for checking routine website design elements for consistency and compliance with standards. They tend to create positive user interface design practices and increase awareness among designers as to the importance of good usability.

However, the feeling within the industry is that these techniques should be considered a complimentary tool to be used in conjunction with traditional Usability

Testing. The online Usability Testing packages provide a benchmark for client-side website performance.

Traditional Usability Testing is likely to be required in order to identify the "in-depth" UI problems and to uncover WHY consumers respond as they do to a user interface as they are trying to complete Tasks.

The programs evaluated generally do not provide a comparison between the correct path(s) to complete a Task with that taken by the Participant. That is, each Task can have one (or more) ideally prescribed routes in order to complete a given Task. The Participant's actual route taken in the test needs to be compared to that ideal route. This "delta" can act as a measure of usability. These programs generally do not provide this insight.

In addition, while the online Usability Testing packages identify potential usability problems, they often do not help by providing a design solution. It is necessary to extrapolate from the human performance numbers obtained to a correction (user interface design modification), and the online UT packages examined are typically light on this need.

These online Usability Testing tools will be of significant value and use to usability professionals and practitioners, but they should be viewed as a supplement to traditional Usability Testing methods. The traditional hands-on techniques of observing consumers using a site and interviewing them with regard to the reasons for their behavior will continue to be a critical component of the usability design effort.

CHAPTER 18

Working with the Institutional Review Board (IRB) at Your Institution

Step 1: Find Out about your IRB and their Requirements

Many research teams that work within a private company do not have to be concerned about meeting the requirements of an Institutional Review Board (IRB). However, most universities and government agencies have Institutional Review Boards, and if you are conducting any kind of research involving human subjects, it is a requirement that you gain approval from that IRB before you begin your research. The IRBs serve a very important purpose of protecting human subjects as individuals participate in all kinds of testing and research. Often, the IRB is located within a department with a title such as Human Subjects Research Office (HSRO), thus find out where the IRB in your institution is located. Some research (for example those involving the testing of a new medication) are more risky than others, and generally speaking, Usability Testing is viewed by most IRBs as a non-invasive, non-threatening type of research and the IRB is likely to treat your application favorably and will grant it approval quickly. Other times the IRB can ask numerous questions and demand numerous clarifications and this can delay your application process for some period of time. One can apply to the IRB for an "Exempt" review status, or for an "Expedited" review status. The "Exempt" classification will result in the quickest approval, and thus you should aim for that type of application if your IRB feels that "Exempt" is the correct classification for your research. One of the "generic" IRBs is the Western Institutional Review Board and it can be found at: www.wirb.com/

Step 2. Get in Touch with your Institutional Review Board

One needs to get in touch with the IRB in their institution and with a "teamwork" approach in mind, find out the specific requirements for an IRB submission and set about giving them all of the information they require.

Step 3: Avoid the Adversarial Approach
One may be tempted to contest what the IRB is requiring of you, particularly because you may have a greater amount of research experience than the examiner reviewing your IRB submission. This approach is not recommended.

Step 4: You Will be Required to Obtain CITI Certification
Your IRB will require that you become CITI certified before they will process your IRB submission. The CITI is a national organization that is used by all IRBs to ensure that researchers have taken a course on the specifics of protecting human subjects while doing research, and one must take the on-line course and become certified before the IRB will accept your submission. CITI stands for "The Collaborative Institutional Training Initiative" and their website can be found at: www.citiprogram.org/

Step 5: Get to Know and Stay in Touch with your IRB Reviewer
While this may vary, typically there is one person who reviews your IRB application and carries it through until the IRB committee votes on your IRB submission. It is a good idea to get to know this person, be able to call them on a first-name basis, and call them up from time to time to check on the progress of your IRB submission. The advantage of this is that your IRB reviewer may have questions, and if you are proactive and get those questions answered in a timely manner, the approval process will be shortened.

Appendix A

A Sample Test Plan

Client Name

Test Plan:
Comparative Usability Testing
of Online Banking Websites

Date

Ergo Research, LLC
Peter P. Mitchell, Ph.D., CHFP
Lesley M. Evans

Purpose:
The purpose of this research is to explore the screen design and ease of navigation of (client's name) online banking service, as compared to two other online banking websites available today. More specifically, when carrying out typical banking Tasks, we will determine which of the three products is the quickest to use and which results in the fewest errors. We will also measure consumer preference over the three sites.

We have outlined below those Tasks and issues that will be included in the test.

Topics to be included in test:
- ➤ Login to Online Banking websites
- ➤ Access specific online account information
- ➤ Setup a payee in order to pay bills online
- ➤ Pay a bill
- ➤ Setup a recurring payment
- ➤ Modify the Personal Profile
- ➤ Navigation to important pages throughout each site

Problem Statement:
During the Usability Test the following problems will be answered:

➤ How does the (client name) online banking website compared to its competitors?
➤ Is the sign-on process user friendly?
➤ Is the language used throughout the website understandable to the end users?
➤ Is the information that is presented to the users in line with their expectations?
➤ Can users navigate through the (client name) online site easily?

User Profile:
The Participants are being recruited as follows:
- Group 1—User has a current Online Banking Account
- Group 2—User doesn't have an Online Banking Account but uses the internet regularly

Number of Test Participants:
20 people are being recruited for the entire study with the expectation of at least 16 people completing the study.
- Group 1—10 people
- Group 2—10 people

Identify User Tasks:
Users will work with the (client name) website as well as 2 other online banking products. The products will be rotated in order of use from user to user.
1. Log on to online banking website
2. What accounts do you have access to through the banking online website?
3. What is your checking account balance?
4. Navigate to create a payee
5. Pay a bill
6. Return to Account summary page
7. Setup a recurring bill (if time permits, may not do on every product)

Generate Material:
➤ Introduction
   The purpose of today's session is to obtain your opinions and reactions to the presentation of functions and features on various online banking websites. You will be asked to login and use each online website to access various account information. I'd like to stress that there are no right or wrong responses here. This is not a test of your skills, but rather your evaluation of the website. We need your honest opinions, both positive and negative, to guide the development of the site. I did not design what you will be seeing, so you can feel comfortable telling me anything you need to about it. These sessions are videotaped

and some of my colleagues are observing from behind the glass, but everything you say is kept confidential. Do you have any questions?

➢ <u>Screener</u>
  ➢ See Attached.

➢ <u>Scenario List</u>
  1. *Overview*
     ➢ Describe Online Banking website
     ➢ Ask about needs and issues with such a system
  2. *Login to website*
➢ Ask what they expect to do during the login on process
  ➢ Ask if they got enough information during the login process
  ➢ Ask what they expect to do after they login
➢ Rate the initial login process
➢ Record success and failures of login
  3. *Complete Task List*
     While completing the Task List the following observations and recording will be made:
➢ Record if users can navigate from one Task to another
➢ Ask what they expect the button commands to do when clicked
➢ Do they know where they are within online banking website?
➢ Can they get back to the home page?

➢ <u>Debriefing</u>
  At the completion of the Task the users will be asked to prioritize each product they would choose for the following:
  1. Which product would you begin using today?
  2. Which product enabled you to comfortably accomplish all of the Tasks important to you?
  3. Which product are you given enough information to complete the necessary Task?
  4. Which product's help is easiest to use?
  5. Which product is easiest to use? Why?
  6. Any comments.

Test Dates:
  • August 17 (9:00am–5:00pm)
  • August 18 (9:00am–5:00pm)

(Session are scheduled for 1.5 hours)

APPENDIX B

Example of a Screener

Screener
(Name of research project)

Hello. This is _____ from _____, a customer research firm. This is not a sales call. May I ask you a few questions? It will only take a couple of minutes and all information will be kept confidential.

Name: _____

Phone: _____

Address: _____

_____

_____

Occupation: _____

1. **Are you working full-time or part-time?** (Quota: At least 50% employed full-time)
   [ ] Full-time   [ ] Home-maker   [ ] Not working (Thank, terminate & tally)
   [ ] Part-time   [ ] Student (Thank, terminate & tally)

2. **Note gender:**
   [ ] Female (Approx. 50%)
   [ ] Male (Approx. 50%)

3. **Have you participated in any market research or usability testing studies in the past 6 months?**
   [ ] Yes (Thank, terminate & tally)
   [ ] No

4. **Do you work for a company in any of the following business areas:**
   • **Marketing research**
   • **A telephone or telecommunications company**
   • **Internet/website design**
   [ ] Yes (Thank, terminate & tally)
   [ ] No

5. **In what range does your age fall?** (Quota: A distribution of ages; Shown are approx. numbers)
   [ ] Under 18 (Thank, terminate & tally)
   [ ] Between 18-24 (3 people)   [ ] Between 45-54 (3 people)
   [ ] Between 25-34 (3 people)   [ ] 55 and over (3 people)
   [ ] Between 35-44 (3 people)

6. **How would you rate your expertise in using the Internet?**
   [ ] Expert, very comfortable in using the Internet
   [ ] Intermediate, can use the Internet comfortably as necessary
   [ ] Novice, I have only used the Internet a few times (Thank, terminate & tally)
   [ ] I don't use the Internet at all, or only very rarely (Thank, terminate & tally)

7. **Have you used the Internet to gather information about a product or service before making a purchase?**
   [ ] Yes
   [ ] No

8. **In the past year, have you used the Internet to purchase products or services?**
   [ ] Yes
   [ ] No (If "No" to both Q7 and Q8, Thank, terminate & tally)

9. **In the past 6 months, have you used the yellow pages?**
   [ ] Yes (If "Yes", ask: [ ] Yellow pages book   [ ] Online yellow pages
   [ ] No (Thank, terminate and tally)

Invitation: We are conducting an important research study, and we would like to get your opinions. We will be holding research sessions on _____ at _____am/pm lasting approximate 1 hr. and 15 minutes. The session will be held at XYZ Market Research facility located at: _____.
This is an opportunity for you to have a say in how a website works. This site will be used by consumers like yourself. In addition, you will receive $75 as our way of saying thanks for your assistance. Would you be able to help us with this research?

Note:
Duration: Approximately 1 hour and 15 minutes; additional 15 minutes between sessions.
Recruit in approximate equal distribution, male/female.
Recruit people with a distribution of occupations.
The research will be conducted at XYZ Market Research facility, Atlanta.

Schedule 1 person/session for the following times, time slots with * will be double sessions with a second respondent being run concurrently in the 1-on-1 testing room.

Those marked with an "#" are two-person sessions. Floaters will not be needed for these sessions.

APPENDIX C

Sample Testing Schedules

- While scheduling may seem like an unimportant item, allotting enough time for each session and scheduling debriefing breaks is a critical part of the Usability Testing process. Use the schedules below as a starting point to set up your testing schedule.

Tuesday, June 12	Wednesday, June 13
8:00 to 9:15 am	8:00 to 9:15 am #
9:30 to 10:45 am	9:30 to 10:45 am
11:00 to 12:15 pm	11:00 to 12:15 pm
Lunch & debriefing session	Lunch & debriefing session
1:15 to 2:30 pm	1:15 to 2:30 pm
Debriefing break—changes?	2:45 to 4:00 pm #
4:15 to 5:30 pm #	4:15 to 5:30 pm #

\# = a two-person test session

Tuesday, April 24	Wednesday, April 25
9:00–10:15	8:00–9:15
10:15–11:30	9:15–10:30
11:30–12:45	Debriefing break
Debriefing break	12:15–1:30
2:30–3:45	1:30–2:45
3:45–5:00	2:45–4:00

APPENDIX D

Sample Tasks

- Below are some example Tasks from past Usability Testing projects.

- Note that each Task requires that the Participant complete some very specific, realistic, measurable activity on the website.

- The Participant completes each Task individually (each Task is given to Participant on a separate sheet of paper), and the Moderator and the observer(s) in the back room monitor and measure the extent to which the Participants can correctly complete each Task.

- The first example is taken from a study for an insurance company. On this website the doctor's office can get information on the current coverage and limits for patients seen by the doctors. It assists doctors' offices in dealing with the insurance company.

Task 1
This website lets you see payments that have been made to your office for claims submitted. You would like to see what you have been paid in the past week. How would you do this?

Task 2
You understand that this website offers courses that will help fulfill your Continuing Education course requirements. You would like to see what is offered. How would you do this?

Task 3
You are interested in locating information on the "Preferred Doctor Provider" program. How would you do this?

Task 4
Susan Jones has just completed her routine checkup and it was found that she needs a MRI scan. You need to find out whether or not she is eligible for an MRI, and what her maximum and deductibles are for this procedure.

Here is her Social Security number: 048-02-7383
How would you do this?

Task 5
You have some free time and would like to begin submitting some of the claims for today's work. Submit two claims.

Task 6
You would like to look up the claims submitted to the insurance company this past December for your practice. How would you do this?

Task 7
You just got a new email address and would like to inform MetLife of this change. Where would you do it on this site?

Another Example of Tasks
- The second example of Tasks is taken from an online telephone look-up study. The Participants were seated at a terminal with the capability of getting information from four different online yellow pages products. These were some of the Tasks we gave them to complete.

Task 1:
You are taking some out-of-town visitors to dinner. They are staying at the Marriott Hotel in downtown Atlanta. You want to take them to a seafood restaurant within 5 miles of the hotel. You want to make sure that the restaurant takes credit cards. Find some restaurants.

Task 2:
Your car needs servicing. Find a Chevrolet dealer near Perimeter Mall. Get a map and driving directions to help you get there.

Task 3:
Your TV set needs repair. It is Saturday. Find a place that is open. Get a map and driving directions.

Task 4:
You are looking for something to do this weekend. Use the "City Guide" or "Going Out" for Atlanta to find some information on whatever you enjoy:

Museums, theater, sporting events. Did you obtain the information you wanted? Was it easy to find?

Task 5:
You need to rent a tuxedo. Since you will have to go to be measured, pick it up, and return it, you would like to find a place near where you work. Find tuxedo rental shops within 10 miles of where you work. Get a map and driving directions to one of them.

Task 6:
Your niece is getting married in June and has asked you to help plan the wedding. Use the "Specialty Guide" to find information about bands that specialize in weddings.

Task 7:
You want to order Chinese food, but you want to try a different restaurant than the one you normally use. Find some of the Chinese restaurants within 5 miles of where you live. Get a map and driving directions.

Task 8:
You want to find a dentist for an 8 year old child. You'd like the dentist to be near Emory University. What are the choices of dentists and what are the hours that a dentist is available?

Task 9:
Your cat has a bad rash and you want to find a doctor that specializes in this. Find one close to your home and get driving directions.

Task 10:
You want to find out the hours of operation of the post office in downtown Atlanta. How would you do this?

Task 11:
Your neighbor's house has termites and she asked you for the name of a company to treat the problem. You recall a company whose name starts with "Term", but you can't remember the full name. Locate a company.

APPENDIX E

Sample Rating Scales

- I normally use a simple rating scale after each Task to quickly find out if the Participant felt that the Task was simple or difficult, given the user interface with which they are working.

- Other rating scales can be used in addition to the primary rating scale—the cautionary note is that the ratings take time, and it is good to keep the Tasks moving quickly. Some usability specialists choose do not use rating scales.

- The benefit of the rating scale data is that, once the study is complete, one can quickly determine if one or more Tasks were particularly difficult in the eyes of the Participants—if so, those are the Tasks that should receive the most user interface re-design effort.

- The rating scale data are also used to corroborate the human performance data obtained through observation.

- The cautionary note: If the process of capturing the rating is lengthy, you run the risk of slowing up or sidetracking the Usability Test. The Usability Test should have a steady pace and a consistent flow—make sure the rating scale activity is brief so as to maintain this flow.

<u>After each Task:</u>

Please rate the ease of carrying out the Task you just completed:

1	2	3	4	5	6	7	8	9	10
Very Difficult									Very Easy

<u>Other rating scales that can be used:</u>

During the Task you just completed, did you always know what to do next?

1	2	3	4	5	6	7	8	9	10

Didn't know   Always knew
what to do next   what to do
                                                               next

How clear was the language used to instruct you in completing this Task?

1	2	3	4	5	6	7	8	9	10

Not clear   Very
at all   Clear

How useful is the capability that was provided in this last Task?

1	2	3	4	5	6	7	8	9	10

Not useful   Very useful

APPENDIX F

Sample Introduction Sheet

Introduction & Instructions

The purpose of today's session is to obtain your opinions and reactions to the presentation of functions and features of an online Dental Provider Portal.

I would like to remind you that we abide by all of the regulations of the Institutional Review Board (the IRB), and one of the provisions in the Consent Form you signed is that at any time during this session, if you feel uncomfortable or if you feel that you do not wish to continue with the research session, you have the right to say that you wish to discontinue. The session will be halted. There will be no negative repercussions toward you whatsoever if you should decide to do so.

Imagine this is the computer you use in your office, the one that you would normally use for your typical daily office tasks. You will be asked to login and use the website to access various insurance information, just as you would do everyday at the office.

You will be asked to imagine yourself in various situations. I'd like to stress that there are no right or wrong responses here. This is not a test of your skills, but rather your evaluation of the website.

We need your honest opinions, both positive and negative, to guide the development of the site. I did not design what you will be seeing, so you can feel comfortable telling me anything you need to about it. As we work with the site today we may come to dead ends, this is not an error on your part, it is because this site is a prototype and not all the functionality is designed.

I will let you know that we reached a dead end and we will continue on. Also, this session is video taped for our research purposes. Are there any questions before we begin?

APPENDIX G

Sample Moderator's Guide and Probe Questions

- Two simple probe questions to ask after each Task:
  1. Was that Task difficult, or easy, to complete? Why?
  2. While completing the Task, was there any point where you were   not sure what to do next?

- These probe questions were used in a case where we were evaluating the look and the initial impression of the homepage of the site.

Initial Reaction to e-Store Home Page

Let's assume you are using the Internet to research wireless phones. You are interested in learning more about (client name) products and services. You have found (client name) Wireless website and are looking at the home page.

1. What would you click on first? Why?

2. Without clicking any of the links, take a moment to look around the home page. Tell me where would you go to find information about:
   - Wireless service
   - Phones and Accessories
   - Prepaid phones

3. Still without clicking, tell me what kind of information you expect to be able to see on the site?

4. Please look at the categories of information available. What are the 3 categories of information of most interest (or most useful) to you?
   - Standard Rate Plans
   - Prepaid
   - Phones
   - Special Offers
   - Buy Accessories

- Customer Service
- Roaming
- View/Pay Your Bill

- **Typical probe questions used after an individual Task.**
  What is your reaction to this screen?
  Explain what this page is about.
  What features are available? (Note: Do they see the top menu bar features?)
  What else do you notice?

  What is your reaction to this Task?
  Is this what you expected?
  Probe column headings? Are they clear?
  What do you think the "clear" button does?

  How do they exit from the site?
  Are they noticing that the table can be sorted?

  Is there anything missing?
  (Note: Did they browse all of the items or use Search function?)
  Did they notice the sort arrows?

- **After all Tasks are done, the Moderator performs a brief interview/discussion intended to capture the user's overall impression. The Moderator asks:**
  1. What do you like/dislike about the e-Store website?
  2. What was the one thing (if any) that you thought was difficult about using the site?
  3. In terms of ease of use, how does the e-Store compare to other websites you use or from which you regularly buy things?
  4. As you were completing the Tasks, did you always know what to do next?
  5. What one thing would you do to improve the ease-of-use of this website?
  6. If you were telling someone else about the site, what is one helpful hint you would provide?

Appendix H

Examples of a Post-test Questionnaire

- This is an example from a Usability Test that was conducted for a software company that was developing a web-based service to enable customers to do online banking.

<u>ABC Software</u>

MoneyScope Usability Testing: Questionnaire

1. Would you use this service? Why or why not? Explain your answer.

2. What is your opinion of doing your banking and managing your finances via the service you just used? What are the pros and cons?

3. Does it make a difference to you if such a service is set up via a direct link to your bank, or if it is set up via the Internet?

4. What other features and capabilities do you think this service should have?

5. What features would make you more likely to use it?

6. As you were completing the Tasks, was it clear to you when you needed to connect to the bank (to get or send information) in order to complete a given Task?

7. Was there any point in completing the Tasks where you were not sure what to do next? When did this occur?

8. What could be done to improve the situation?

9. What <u>one</u> thing would you do to improve the way this service works? What else?

10. If the Participant was doing a comparison Usability Test of Version A vs. Version B a final question would be, Overall, which Version did you prefer, A or B? Why did you make this selection?

APPENDIX I

An Example Executive Summary in a Report

It is often the case that the only thing that is read is the Executive Summary. Therefore, the Executive Summary must be brief and crystal clear as to the findings of the Usability Test.

Prioritize the findings and issues; present the most important findings (the changes that <u>have</u> to be made) first. If there are one or two things that a manager glancing over the report must take away with them, make sure those findings/issues are very salient.

Here is an Executive Summary from one of my reports, with client identification modified to maintain confidentiality.

Executive Summary
- Usability Testing of the most recent design for the new XYZ website was conducted in Chicago on August 14 and 15, 2001. A total of 20 test Participants were included in the test. They were given several "real world" look-up Tasks to complete. The researchers monitored their performance in completing the Tasks (any errors to aspects of the site that were confusing) and the research Moderators probed the test consumers for their preferences with regard to the look and feel, as well as the functioning of the website. Examples of web pages examined in this test are given throughout this report.

- <u>Most Important Finding</u>: The results page shows the "Featured Businesses" list first, followed by the "All Businesses" list lower on the page. **This was confusing** to people in the test. It was not clear that the Featured Businesses are the advertisers. People in this test thought that the Featured Businesses list was the actual list showing the results of their search. These featured businesses listings should look very different from the alphabetical listing showing all businesses. Perhaps the section should be called "Displayed Advertisers". Also, there should be a button at the beginning of the featured

90

businesses section saying: "See All Businesses List" to enable the consumer to quickly get to the full list.

- A user interface difficulty uncovered in the previous test was that consumers tended to fill in data for both business category <u>and</u> business name. The new design makes it clearer that the user should provide one or the other piece of information. There were few difficulties with this part of the Task with the new web page design.

- There were, however, some test Participants who **did not see the Business Name search section**, which is lower on the page. People said that the heading did not stand out. The section should be slightly higher on the page and the heading should be larger.

- The left nav area is brighter and more attention-getting than the main search area—this is a problem. It is suggested that the main search area have the **more prominent look.**

- The **banner ad** on the homepage should be at the **bottom** of the page; this results in less confusion for the consumer. On the results page the banner ad should be at the very top of the page. All banner **ads should be set off** by some white space or background shading to visually differentiate the ads from other data on the page.

- The way in which the consumer sees the list of categories was examined in this test. One way uses a pull-down list, the other presenting all of the categories at once. People tended to **prefer seeing all of the categories at once,** however, if this takes additional time, the pull-down approach should be used.

- On the results/listings page people in the test did not immediately see the critical information about the search, which is presented at the top of the page (number of listings, category, and market). This information **should be more prominent.**

- Some people did not see the "Modify This Search" button. It is suggested that **three separate buttons** for modifying the search be presented at the top of the results page: (a) narrow by zip code, (b) narrow by town or suburb, (c) narrow by landmark.

APPENDIX J

Sample Video Permission &
Confidentiality Form

Confidentiality Form

Thank you for taking the time to participate in this important research study. Please be aware that information will be provided to you that (client company) does not to be released to the public.

It is very important that you do not disclose the information that you may obtain as a result of your participation in this study. In addition, we will be videotaping your research session so that other people with (client company) who could not be here today can benefit from your comments. These videotapes will be used only for our research purposes; your comments and opinions are kept confidential.

Please read the two statements below and sign this form where indicated.

I agree that I will disclose no information to any person or corporation about the product research being conducted today on behalf of (client company).

I understand that videotape and audiotape recordings will be made and I grant (client company) the right to use this tape for the research purposes stated above. I waive my right to review the tape prior to its use by (client company).

Signature: _____

Please print name: _____

Date: _____

APPENDIX K

Code of Ethics When Conducting Usability Testing

The following Code of Ethics is taken from the "1993 Human Factors and Ergonomics Society Directory and Yearbook", © 1993 by the Human Factors and Ergonomics Society, Inc. All rights reserved.

Article IV. Subject Precautions

Human factors scientists and engineers have the responsibility of treating both human and animal Participants humanely and in accordance with federal, state, and local laws or regulations, as well as the generally accepted procedures within the scientific community.

Principle 1
Members determine through consultation with colleagues or institutional review committees, that the exposure of human or animal research Participants to hazards, stress, divulgence of history or preferences, or tedium is commensurate with the significance of the problem being researched.

Principal 2
Members determine the degree of hazard present in the exposure of human or animal research Participants, avoiding any exposures to human Participants that may result in death, dismemberment, permanent dysfunction or extreme pain, and utilize the lowest levels of exposure to both human and animal Participants consistent with the phenomenon under consideration.

Principal 3
Members ensure the ethical treatment of human and animal research Participants by collaborators, assistants, students, and employees.

Principal 4
Members establish an informed consent when required by institutional, state, or federal codes or regulations, making explicit in plain language the language the

terms of participation, particularly with respect to any elements of risk or stress involved, and adhere to those terms throughout the experiment. One of these terms must be that the subject has the right to terminate participation at any time without prejudice.

Principal 5

Members do not coerce potential human research Participants to participate as Participants, nor do they use undue monetary rewards to induce Participants to take risks they would not otherwise take.

Principal 6

Members preserve the confidentiality of any information obtained from human research Participants that, if divulged, may have harmful effects on those Participants.

[Note: Please go to "IRB", "HSRO", and "CITI" via one of the search engines to get a list of other code of ethics requirements from these organizations whenever one is conducting research with human subjects.]

APPENDIX L

List of
Professional Societies

Usability Professionals' Association (UPA)
230 E. Ohio Street
Suite 400
Chicago, IL 60611-3265
312-596-5298
www.upassoc.org

Human Factors and Ergonomics Society (HFES)
P.O. Box 1369
Santa Monica, CA 90406
310-394-1811

Society for Technical Communication (STC)
901 N. Stuart Street
Suite 904
Arlington, VA 22203-1822
703-522-4114
www.stc.org
stc@stc.org

Qualitative Research Consultants Association (QRCA)
P.O. Box 2396
Gaithersburg, MD 20886-2396
301-391-6644
www.qrca.org
qrca@qrca.org

SIG Computer-Human Interaction (SIG-CHI)
1515 Broadway
New York, N.Y. 10036-5701
800-342-6626
www.sigchi.org

APPENDIX M

List of
Usability Testing Consultants

- You may determine that you need assistance in either conducting your Usability Testing sessions, or in interpreting the findings and modifying the design of your user interface.

- I am able to assist you with these services. I can be contacted at:
    Peter Mitchell, Ph.D.
    520 Brickell Key Drive
    Unit 1701
    Miami, FL 33131-2660
    305-677-3442
    mitchellmiami@yahoo.com

- In addition, there are many very capable usability consultants located around the country, and I would like to provide you with a list of these consultants, whom you may draw upon as needed.

Firm	Location	Contact	Phone
Tech-Ed, Inc.	Palo Alto, CA	Stephanie Rosenbaum	650-493-1010
Usable Solutions	Colorado	Karen Seidler-Patterson	719-487-0563
Simply Usable Through Design	Dallas/Ft.Worth, TX	Janice James	817-460-2192
Snyder Consulting	Salem, NH	Carolyn Snyder	603-890-2411
Performance Research & Design	Brewster, NY	Nick Simonelli	845-279-5099
Redish & Associates	Bethesda, MD	Ginny Redish	301-229-3039
Mauro New Media	New York, NY	Chuck Mauro	212-343-2878
Ergo Soft Laboratories	Austin, TX		512-372-8684
Dray & Associates	Minneapolis, MN	Susan Dray	612-377-1980
Arbor Comm	Ann Arbor, MI		734-996-9016
Behavioristics, Inc.	Los Angeles, CA	Heather Desurvire	310-823-6543
Optavia	Madison, WI		800-218-4671
The Usability Group	Morganville, NJ		877-884-0300
Weinschenk Group	Edgar, WI	Susan Weinschenk	800-236-2599

APPENDIX N

List of Resources for Recruiting Participants & Renting a Testing Facility

- You can save money by doing the recruiting yourself and by conducting the Usability Testing in a conference room at your offices.

- However, many people prefer to use an outside service to help with either one or both of these Tasks.

- You may use a service to recruit the Participants, but then hold the testing at your own offices, and thus, save significantly on the cost of renting a research facility.

- Given below is a list of research organizations that can conduct the recruiting for you and provide a facility (with a receptionist, testing room, observation room, one-way mirror, etc.) where you can carry out your Usability Testing.

- This list is but a small sample of all of the available research organizations across the United States. Research organizations are also available in most countries throughout the world. However, only U.S. firms are listed here. For a complete list of research organizations in the U.S. and the world, please contact one of these research industry trade groups:

Research Industry Groups
1. Quirks Marketing Research
   P.O. Box 23536
   Minneapolis, MN 55423
   952-854-5101
   info@quirks.com
   www.quirks.com

2. The Green Book
    American Marketing Association
    P.O. Box 837
    Hartsdale, N.Y. 10530
    914-761-0199

3. The Blue Book
    Marketing Research Association
    111 E. Wacker Drive, Suite 600
    Chicago, IL 60601
    312-644-6610

Research Firms & Test Facilities

Atlanta, GA
Jackson Associates
1140 Hammond Drive
Building H
Atlanta, GA 30340
770-394-8702

Focus on Atlanta
3953 Pleasantdale Road, Suite 110
Atlanta, GA 30340
770-447-9800

Boston, MA
Bernett Focus Group Center
1505 Commonwealth Avenue
Boston, MA 02135
617-254-1314

Fieldwork—Boston
The Prudential Tower
Prudential Center
Boston, MA 02199
617-899-3660

Chicago, IL
Fieldwork, Inc.
500 Michigan Avenue, Suite 1200
Chicago, IL 60611
800-863-4353

Smith Research
150 E. Huron, Suite 1010
Chicago, IL 60611
847-948-0440

Cincinnatti, OH
Integrated Research Associates
708 Walnut Avenue, Suite 800
Cincinnatti, OH 45202
513-361-2700

Dallas/Ft. Worth
Common Knowledge
16200 Dallas Parkway, Suite 140
Dallas, TX 75248
800-710-9147

Dallas Focus
511 E. John Carpenter Freeway, Suite 100
Irving, TX 75062
972-869-2366

Denver, CO
Strategic Insights
3967 E. Garnet Way
Littleton, CO 80126-5062
303-683-9200

Ft. Lauderdale, FL
Mars Research
1700 N. University Drive, Suite 205
Coral Springs, FL 33071
954-755-2805

Houston, TX
CQS Research
2500 West Loop S., Suite 300
Houston, TX 77027
800-460-9111

Los Angeles, CA
Adler-Weiner Research
10990 Wilshire Blvd., Suite 200
Los Angeles, CA 90024
310-440-2330

Assistance In Marketing
11175 Santa Monica Blvd., Suite 700
Los Angeles, CA 90025
800-308-3575

Miami, FL
Target Market Research
4990 S.W. 72nd Avenue, Suite 110
Miami, FL 33155-5524
800-500-1492

Milwaukee, WI
The Dieringer Research Group, Inc.
3064 N. 78th Street
Milwaukee, WI 53222
800-489-4540

Philadelphia, PA
Plaza Research
2 Greentree Centre
Marlton, NJ 08053
609-596-7777

Philadelphia Focus
111 North 17th Street, 3rd Floor
Philadelphia, PA 19103
215-561-5500

Phoenix, AZ
Focus Market Research
Camelback Executive Park
6991 E. Camelback Road, Suite D118
Phoenix, AZ 85251
480-874-2714

WestGroup Research
2720 E. Thomas, Bldg. A
Phoenix, AZ 85016
800-999-1200

Portland, OR
Focus Portland
4915 S.W. Griffin Drive, Suite 210
Beaverton, OR 97005
503-350-4829

Salt Lake City, UT
iResearch
4482 W. Bingham Park Drive
West Jordan, UT 84088
801-280-9399

San Francisco, CA
Consumer Research Associates
111 Pine Street, 17th Floor
San Francisco, CA 94111
800-800-5055

Ecker & Associates
220 S. Spruce Avenue, Suite 100
South San Francisco, CA 94080-4404
650-871-6800

St. Louis, MO
Delve
1355 N. Highway Drive
Fenton, MO 63099
800-325-3338

Washington, DC
Metro Research Services, inc.
9990 Lee Highway
Suite 110
Fairfax, VA 22030
703-385-1108

Shugoll Research
7475 Wisconsin Avenue
Suite 200
Bethesda, MD 20814
301-656-0310

Appendix O

Acknowledgements

First, and most importantly, I would like to thank my wife, Marilynn, and acknowledge her many hours and significant help in compiling and writing this book.

In addition, over the 25 years I have been performing usability research, I have been fortunate to have been associated with a number of very talented people who have provided a great deal of assistance in conducting the Usability Testing sessions for Ergo Research, LLC.

I would like to thank them for the tireless hours poured into the various Usability Testing programs we conducted and for their insights into the user interface design changes required to improve the ease-of-use of our clients' products and services.

Many thanks to each of these people for their assistance: Gail Blazieski, Kristi Buynak, Ann Canby, Ed Christi, Lesley Evans, Beth Giurelli, Nancy Herdegen, Charles Keating, Brian Lazalow, Elizabeth Mallen, Robert Olman, Mark O'Shaughnessy, Joel Raphael, Toby Sanders, Roberta Shea, Peter Stanz, Lisa Stiefelman, and Isabel Walcott.

APPENDIX P

Bio for the Author

Peter P. Mitchell, Ph.D., CHFP

Peter received his Ph.D. in Human Factors from Stevens Institute of Technology, Hoboken, New Jersey in 1982. He received his MA in Experimental Psychology from Victoria University of Wellington, Wellington, New Zealand in 1975. Peter received his BA in Psychology from Lafayette College, Easton, Pennsylvania in 1972.

He began work in the field of human factors as Research Associate at Human Factors/Industrial Design, New York City, from 1977 to 1981. In 1981 he founded Ergo Research LLC. He has been providing Usability Testing, human factors, customer experience management, and market research services to Fortune 500 companies since 1981. A partial list of clients is given at the bottom of this page.

He received his CHFP (Certified Human Factors Professional) certification from the Board of Certification in Professional Ergonomics in 1992. He is Past President of the Metropolitan Chapter of the Human Factors & Ergonomics Society.

Peter currently serves as Interim President of The New York City Chapter of the Usability Professionals' Association.

Peter has received two patents relating to human factors: Patent # 5,651,053 and Patent # 4,711,033.

He is a Research Assistant Professor at the University of Miami, Miller School of Medicine, and works in The Center for Patient Safety within University of Miami/Jackson Memorial Hospital in Miami, Florida. He also works in the William Lehman Injury Research Center, which is also within the University of Miami.

Peter continues his consulting business, Ergo Research, LLC in Miami. A partial list of past clients of Ergo Research LLC include: The American Stock Exchange, ADP, Alcatel, AT&T, Bank of America, BellSouth, Bellcore, Chase Manhattan Bank, Cingular, Citibank, Cox Communications, Datascope, Dept. of Homeland Security, Discover Card, Hewlett-Packard, IBM, James-River Paper Co., Kodak, Met Life, Motorola, Nextel, NYNEX, Panasonic, Pitney-Bowes, Spacelabs, Time-Warner, Timex, and Verizon.

APPENDIX Q

Workshop At Your Company

- You may wish to get Usability Testing started at your company, but don't know where to start.

- I provide a 2-day workshop: "Running Usability Tests At Your Company: A Training Program".

- It covers:
  o How to scope the problem
  o How to design a Usability Test
  o Training the Moderator
  o Collecting the data
  o Interpreting the results
  o Applying findings to improve the UI

- Just the things you need to know. Get Usability Testing up and running at your company. For more information: p.mitchell@miami.edu

APPENDIX R

References

Bias, Randolph and Mayhew, Deborah (eds.) Cost-Justifying Usability. Morgan Kaufman Publishers, San Francisco, 1994.

Dumas, Joseph. "Usability Testing Methods: Think-aloud Protocols", in Design By People For People: Essays on Usability, Russell J. Branaghan, ed., Usability Professionals' Association, Chicago, IL, 2001.

Dumas, Joseph. "How Many Participants in a Usability Test Are Enough?", in Design By People By People: Essays on Usability, Russell J. Branaghan, ed., Usability Professionals' Association, Chicago, IL, 2001.

Dumas, Joseph. "Usability Testing Methods: Subjective Measures—Measuring Attitudes and Opinions", in Design By People For People: Essays on Usability, Russell J. Branaghan, ed., Usability Professionals' Association, Chicago, IL, 2001.

Dumas, Joseph and Redish, Janice. A Practical Guide to Usability Testing. Ablex Publishing, 1993.

Dumas, Joseph. Designing User Interfaces for Software. Prentice Hall, Inc., Englewood Cliffs, N.J., 1988

Fleming, Jennifer. Web Navigation: Designing the User Experience. O'Reilly & Associates, Inc., Sebastopol, CA, 1998.

Krug, Steve. Don't Make Me Think: A Common Sense Approach to Web Usability. New Riders Publishing, Indianapolis, IN, 2000.

Nielsen, Jakob. Designing Web Usability. New Riders Publishing, Indianapolis, IN, 2000.

Nielsen, Jakob and Tahir, Marie. Homepage Usability. New Riders Publishing, Indianapolis, IN, 2002.

Pearrow, Mark. <u>Website Usability Handbook</u>. Charles River Media, Inc., Rockland, MA, 2000.

Rubin, Jeffrey. <u>Handbook of Usability Testing.</u> John Wiley & Sons, Inc., New York, NY, 1994.

Shneiderman, Ben. <u>Designing the User Interface: Strategies for Effective Human-Computer Interaction</u>. Addison-Wesley Publishing, New York, NY, 1998.

Spool, Jared, et al. <u>Website Usability: A Designer's Guide</u>. Morgan Kaufmann Publishers, Inc., San Francisco, CA, 1999.

Tamler, Howard. "How (Much) To Intervene in a Usability Testing Session", in <u>Design By People For People: Essays on Usability</u>, Russell J. Branaghan, ed., Usability Professionals' Association, Chicago, IL, 2001.

Vora, Pawan. "Classifying User Errors in Human-Computer Interactive Tasks", in <u>Design By People For People: Essays on Usability</u>, Russell J. Branaghan, ed., Usability Professionals' Association, Chicago, IL, 2001.

Vredenburg, Karel, Isensee, Scott, and Righi, Carol. <u>User-Centered Design</u>. Prentice-Hall PTR, Upper Saddle River, NJ, 2002.

978-0-595-42276-0
0-595-42276-4

儿童情绪管理与性格培养绘本

I CAN KEEP MY WORD

我是诚实守信
的好孩子

胡媛媛 编

广东旅游出版社
GUANGDONG TRAVEL & TOURISM PRESS
中国·广州

图书在版编目（ＣＩＰ）数据

我是诚实守信的好孩子 / 胡媛媛编. — 广州：广东旅游出版社，2016.11
（儿童情绪管理与性格培养绘本）
ISBN 978-7-5570-0554-2

Ⅰ.①我… Ⅱ.①胡… Ⅲ.①儿童故事 – 图画故事 – 中国 – 当代 Ⅳ.①I287.8

中国版本图书馆 CIP 数据核字(2016)第 237794 号

总 策 划：罗艳辉
责任编辑：殷如筠
封面绘图：赵里骏
责任技编：刘振华
责任校对：李瑞苑

我 是 诚 实 守 信 的 好 孩 子
WO SHI CHENGSHI SHOUXIN DE HAO HAIZI

广东旅游出版社出版发行

（广州市越秀区建设街道环市东路 338 号银政大厦西楼 12 楼　　邮编：510030）
邮购电话：020-87348243
广东旅游出版社图书网
www.tourpress.cn
湖北楚天传媒印务有限责任公司
（湖北省武汉市东湖新技术开发区流芳园横路 1 号　　邮编：430205）
787 毫米 × 1092 毫米　16 开　2 印张　1 千字
2016 年 11 月第 1 版第 1 次印刷
定价：15.00 元

秋天到了，院子里的小树苗被
风爷爷吹弯了腰。

In fall, the little trees in the yard
bent over in the wind.

小树苗这么娇弱,它们怎么过冬呢?心灵手巧的小猫咪对小树苗说:"让我为你织一条漂亮的围巾吧!"

The little trees were so weak. How could they survive the winter?

"Let me weave a beautiful scarf for you!" a sweet and smart kitten said to a tree.

"谢谢你,小猫咪!"小树苗随风摇摆着,感激地向小猫咪道谢。

"Thank you, kitten!" the swaying tree said to the kitten.

小猫咪从商店里买来毛线，开始努力地编织围巾。

The kitten bought some wool at a store and started to weave a scarf.

天黑了,月亮挂在树梢上,柔和的灯光透过窗户,小猫咪还在编织着围巾。

It was dark. The moon was hanging above the tree. Soft lighting poured in through the windows. The kitten was still weaving the scarf.

天亮了，"啊……"小猫咪打了个哈欠，手上仍然没停。

At dawn, "ah..." the kitten yawned but did not stop weaving.

窗外，一群小伙伴正在踢足球，他们趴在窗前说："小猫咪，快和我们一起玩吧。"
"对不起，我要给小树苗织围巾，不能玩！"

The kitten's friends were playing soccer outside the window. "Kitten, let's play together," they said. "Sorry, I can't play. I must weave the scarf for the little tree."

9

"天气这么暖和，哪里需要围巾？"可不是嘛，
天气这么温暖，冬天还远着呢！

"It's very warm, what do you need a scarf for?"
Well, it was still warm, and the winter was far away!

小猫咪和小伙伴们一起踢足球，
玩得满头大汗，快乐极了。

The kitten was playing soccer with friends
and sweating heavily. They had a lot of fun.

傍晚时分，"哗啦啦……"下雨了，小树苗的满头秀发被雨水打落下来，只剩下光秃秃的枝丫。

At nightfall, the rain was pouring down. The little tree's leaves were torn down by the rain, left only bare branches.

"我真不应该贪玩，忘了对小树苗的承诺。"小猫咪怀着愧疚的心情，继续编织围巾。

"Oh, I shouldn't have played and forgotten my promise!" The kitten was ashamed and continued to weave.

"小猫咪，歇歇吧，看你的眼睛都熬红了！"猫妈妈摸着小猫咪的头说。小猫咪也想歇一歇，但是想到对小树苗的承诺，她一刻也不敢停歇。

"Just have a rest, my kitten. Look at your red eyes!" Mom said, stroking kitten's head gently. The kitten would like to rest, but she couldn't stop weaving when thinking of her promise to the little tree.

冬天来得真快啊，雪花飘飘洒洒地从天上落下来。小树苗在寒风中冻得瑟瑟发抖。

The winter came so soon. Snowflakes were dancing in the air, and the little tree was shivering.

"不能歇，不能歇。不能让小树苗冻坏了。"小猫咪继续织呀织，围巾终于织好了。

"Keep weaving, keep weaving! I must protect the little tree from severe cold." Kitten was weaving unceasingly, and finally the scarf was done.

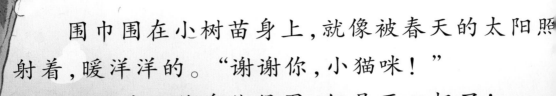

围巾围在小树苗身上，就像被春天的太阳照射着，暖洋洋的。"谢谢你，小猫咪！"

小猫咪虽然身体很累，但是开心极了！

Wearing the scarf, the little tree was as warm as in the spring sunshine. "You are appreciated, Kitten!"
The kitten was so tired but yet very happy!

"说到就做到，你真是一个诚实守信的好孩子！"妈妈对小猫咪竖起大拇指夸赞道。

"You have kept your words, my child. I'm proud of your honesty and credibility!" mother cat gave Kitten a thumbs up and praised.

小猫咪拖着疲惫的身体，钻进温暖的
被窝里慢慢睡去。

Kitten was exhausted and fell
asleep slowly in her warm bed.

她做了一个甜美的梦：小树苗长成了参天大树，一阵微风吹过，它发出"沙沙"的声音，似乎在对小猫咪表示感谢呢！

She had a sweet dream: the little tree had grown into a towering tree, rustling in the wind and saying "thank you" to Kitten.

给父母的话：

自古以来，诚信就是为人处事之本，也是每个人必备的素质。只有拥有诚信的宝贵品德，才能在竞争激烈的现代社会立足。

诚信教育对于孩子来说，尤为重要，因为孩子正处于人生的美好开端，还未定性，极易受到外界的影响。就像故事中的小猫，被小伙伴们一怂恿，就违背了自己的承诺，直到认识到自己的做法大错特错，才醒悟过来。所有美好的品质都应该在孩童时期打下基础，家长应该坚持诚信教育，在生活中避免孩子受到不诚信的人或事物的影响。

为了培养孩子诚实守信的品质，首先，家长们应该以身作则，言传身教，为孩子做出表率；其次，家长们要耐心、细心地把诚信教育深入到日常生活中去，通过孩子遇到的具体事例来有力地证明诚信的重要性。

当然，在书籍的海洋中，讲述诚信的故事俯拾即是，与孩子共同阅读这些有关诚信的故事，讨论其中蕴含的道理，也是很有必要的。因此我们精心编著了本册绘本，希望以有趣的故事、精美的图画，潜移默化地使小朋友理解诚信的意义，鞭策自己成长为一个诚实守信的孩子，一个能承担起别人信任的人。